USBORNE ILLUSTRATED GUIDE TO NORSE MYTHS AND LEGENDS

Cheryl Evans and Anne Millard

Designed and illustrated by Rodney Matthews

CONTENTS

Additional design by Graham Round

Additional illustration by Joe McEwan, Mark Duffin and Jan Nesbitt

Consultant checker Chris Jackson

BEFORE YOU START

This book is an introduction to the most famous gods and goddesses in Norse Mythology and their exploits. There are many more myths than there is room to include here, but the book will give you a taste of the fantasy world of the Norse gods.

About this book

The gods are introduced on pages 10-21 and you will find the best-known stories about them on pages 22-39.

To help you understand the people who told the myths, you can find out about the history and religion of the Norsemen on pages 4-7. The map on page 3 shows their travels.

Starting on page 40 is a detailed Who's Who reference section of characters and monsters that appear in the myths. In the book their names appear in bold print the first time they occur in a story. Use the Who's Who to find out about Trolls, Dwarfs, Elves and other creatures or to find characters for your own role-playing games.

What is a myth?

It is difficult to define exactly what a myth is. It is usually considered to be a work of the imagination that has a religious significance. Some appear to try to explain things which would probably be described scientifically today, such as how the world began.

Others describe the gods' behaviour, which was an exaggerated version of the lifestyle of the Norsemen and may have been meant to inspire courage. It is impossible at this distance of time to know exactly why particular gods were worshipped.

Where the myths came from

In this book the Norse Myths are taken to be mainly from Scandinavia and Iceland, although Norsemen also lived in Germany, Russia and further afield (see map opposite). People in different areas created local myths of their own.

The only myth in this book that was not wholly Scandinavian is the story of **Sigurd** and the Nibelungs (see pages 34-35). This came from Germany, but was adopted by the Scandinavians. It is famous due to Richard Wagner's opera cycle, *Der Ring des Nibelungen*.

How the myths were told

The Norse Myths were passed on by word of mouth. There were people who were especially good at telling them, called bards. They would entertain the lords in their halls on the long, winter evenings.

The myths were often composed as poems, which probably helped the bards to remember them. Those that were in prose were called sagas.

They were told in a typically Norse style, using tricks such as putting words with a similar sound together to create an effect.

There were traditional ways to describe each god, which came up again and again.

Characters had lots of nicknames – **Odin,** king of the gods, had as many as fifty, such as One-Eyed and Allfather.

The Norsemen were very keen on their ancestry. Long lists of heroes were often included in the stories. Objects were often given names, too.

MAP OF EUROPE

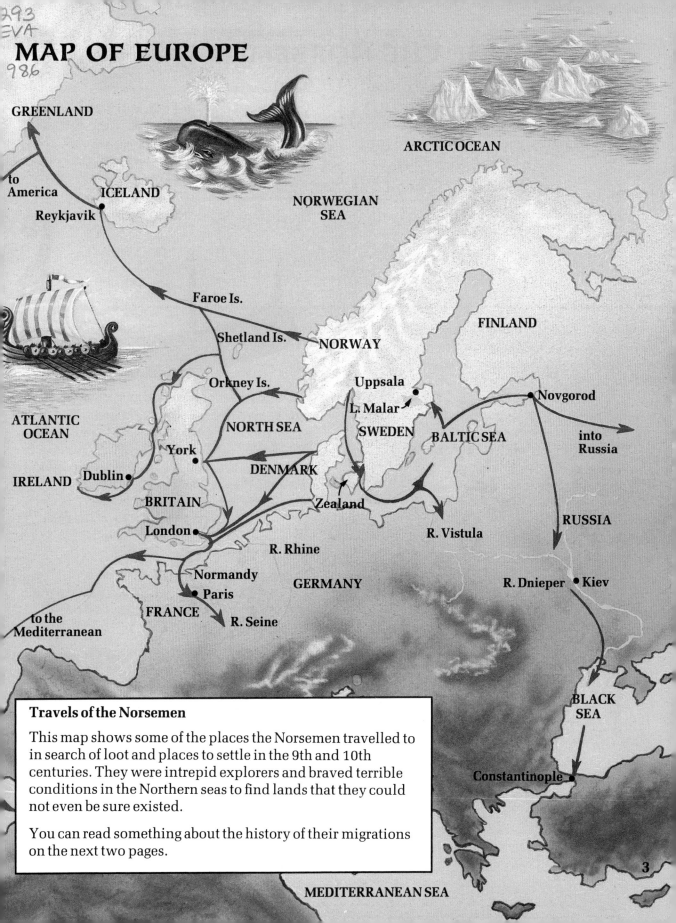

293
EVA
986

GREENLAND

to America

ICELAND

Reykjavik

ARCTIC OCEAN

NORWEGIAN SEA

Faroe Is.

Shetland Is.

FINLAND

NORWAY

ATLANTIC OCEAN

Orkney Is.

Uppsala

L. Malar

Novgorod

into Russia

NORTH SEA

York

SWEDEN

BALTIC SEA

IRELAND

Dublin

DENMARK

BRITAIN

Zealand

RUSSIA

London

R. Vistula

R. Rhine

Normandy

GERMANY

R. Dnieper

Kiev

Paris

FRANCE

to the Mediterranean

R. Seine

BLACK SEA

Constantinople

Travels of the Norsemen

This map shows some of the places the Norsemen travelled to in search of loot and places to settle in the 9th and 10th centuries. They were intrepid explorers and braved terrible conditions in the Northern seas to find lands that they could not even be sure existed.

You can read something about the history of their migrations on the next two pages.

3

MEDITERRANEAN SEA

HISTORY OF THE NORSEMEN

The Norsemen did not use writing until very late in their history. They passed their myths on by word of mouth for centuries until they were written down by people such as the Icelander Snorri Sturlusson in the 12th century AD. By this time, Iceland had become Christian and the new religion probably influenced how Snorri told the ancient sagas. Below you can read about the beginnings of the Norsemen.

The Germani

About 1000 BC, there was a group of tribes in North-West Europe who shared similar languages and customs. At one time they were probably all closely related and may have come from further east. They slowly spread into South Scandinavia, the Baltic islands, Jutland and the North German Plain. The wider apart they spread, the more different they became.

This is a Runestone. Runes were magic symbols that were the earliest Norse form of writing.

The history of these people is not well-known because they did not record it. What we do know about them is mostly from Roman accounts. These are usually unfavourable, as the Romans considered the tribes to be barbaric enemies. They lumped all the tribes together and called them 'Germani', although there were really three distinct groups:

East Germani

These tribes lived around the River Vistula (see map on page 3). They included the Goths, Visigoths and Vandals. They migrated towards the Black Sea and came up against the Romans in the 4th century AD.

West Germani

These people spread south and west towards the Rivers Rhine and Danube. They clashed with the Romans in the 2nd century AD. They were the ancestors of the Germans, the Franks who populated parts of France, and the Angles and Saxons who later invaded Britain.

North Germani or Vikings

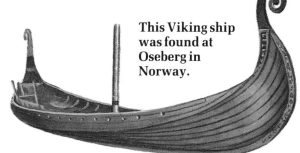

This Viking ship was found at Oseberg in Norway.

Another group moved north into Scandinavia and became the North or Norse men. The period of their history between about the years AD 700 and 1070 is often called the Viking Era and the Norsemen at this time are known as Vikings. Viking is a Norse word, whose meaning is not clear, but it may refer to the adventurous, seafaring lifestyle of the time.

The Viking life

Norsemen were originally farmers and fishermen but the lands they inhabited were so rugged and infertile that they had to find other means to live.

Traders used sledges like this one.

They were expert sailors and some of them became rich through trading. Others hired themselves out to foreign kings – the Emperors of Constantinople were proud of their Viking bodyguard, called the Varangian Guard.

Some found the rich monasteries on the Scottish islands and the coasts of England and Ireland too tempting and turned to piracy. They terrorized the coasts and gained a bloodthirsty reputation.

This is the handle of a Viking sword.

The spread of the Norsemen

The Vikings soon spread further west looking for conquests. They reached Iceland (AD 874), Greenland (AD 982) and even North America (about AD 1000). They explored via the rivers of Europe too, into France, Germany, Russia and as far as Constantinople. The riches of the Mediterranean cities also invited Viking raids.

Viking raiders and traders started to settle in the lands they visited and often made their mark where they settled. A Dane called Canute became King of England between AD 1016 and 1035. Another, Rollo, was made a duke in France. His duchy was Normandy, meaning North men's land.

These are Viking coins from York in England.

The importance of Iceland

Iceland left its mark in the Norse Myths because this is where they were first written down. The main sources are the works known as the *Verse Edda* and the *Prose Edda*. The *Verse Edda* consists of poems about the myths by different poets. The *Prose Edda* is the work of Snorri Sturlusson, who lived from 1179-1241. It is a guide for poets and includes many of the myths.

The Icelandic landscape and climate seem to have had an influence on the myths. The extremes of ice and fire that appear in the stories recall the snow and ice, volcanoes and hot geysers of Iceland.

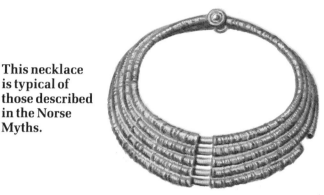

This necklace is typical of those described in the Norse Myths.

The coming of Christianity

Christianity took a long time to reach these northern tribes. Missionaries first appeared in Denmark in the 9th century AD and the word took about 200 years to spread. As Christianity was accepted, so the old gods and goddesses died out.

By the end of the 11th century AD the Norsemen had stopped their Viking activities and become part of the pattern of Medieval Europe in the kingdoms of Norway, Sweden and Denmark.

This early Christian church still stands at Heddal, in Norway. It is made of wood and is called a stave church. It is thought that the pagan temples of the Vikings may have been built in a similar way.

MYTHS AND RELIGION

The Norse Myths are stories concerning the gods of the Norsemen, and formed part of their religion. They illustrate the behaviour that was admired or condemned by the gods, although they do not provide definite rules or guidelines as in religious works like the Bible or the Koran.

The gods and goddesses

Freyja was goddess of love and beauty. This pendant is an image of her.

This is a carved memorial stone. It shows Odin, King of the gods, with his servants the Valkyries. Below them is a Viking ship.

What religion meant to the Norsemen

It is hard to know exactly what the gods meant to the Vikings, or how they worshipped them, since they did not write anything down. They built temples, but very few remains have been found as they were made of wood and only the foundations have survived.

Outsiders who came into contact with them gave horrified reports of animal and even human sacrifices, but they seem to have made no effort to understand the meaning of the ceremonies.

This richly carved wooden cart may have been used in religious ceremonies.

We do know that there was a large number of gods and goddesses, divided into two types, the **Aesir** and the **Vanir.** They represented different aspects of life and people worshipped whichever ones were most relevant to them.

The Vanir were fertility gods and important to farmers, while the Aesir were warriors, worshipped by fighting men and kings. Some people think that the Vanir were the first Norse gods and that the Aesir were introduced later. The myth about the war between the gods (see page 22) may represent the struggle for popularity between the two types.

Apart from temples, natural places such as a clearing, a waterfall or a stone were sometimes dedicated to a god.

What the gods were like

The Norse gods were very like the Norsemen. They fought, married and loved adventures. They felt human emotions such as jealousy and could behave in a most ungodlike way.

They were not immortal which meant they could be truly heroic since their lives could be in danger. In fact, most of them are doomed to die at **Ragnarok**, or the end of the world (see page 38).

Here is a bronze statue of Thor the thunder god.

Giants, Trolls and Dwarfs

Apart from the gods, the Norsemen believed the world was populated by all sorts of strange creatures, some good and some evil. **Elves** inhabited almost every wood and stream and could be mischievous or helpful. **Dwarfs** lived underground and it was said that they could

The god Thor was famous for his hammer. Pendants like this one were worn to ward off evil spirits.

not stand the daylight. If they were caught outside at dawn they turned to stone, which explains the scattered rocks on the valley floors. **Kobolds** were small human-shaped creatures who frequented barns and stables and could be helpful if treated well.

Trolls and **Giants** were both very large and dangerous and lived in the mountains.

Priests and seeresses

There were priests and priestesses who were thought to have special powers to talk to the gods, but most religious rites could be performed by chiefs or kings when necessary. The religion does not appear to have had fixed ceremonies and priests and priestesses were not set aside from ordinary people.

This bronze statue wearing a horned helmet came from Zealand. It is probably of one of the gods.

There were also women who went into trances and claimed to speak directly from the gods. They were called seeresses and travelled the country with women companions, prophesying.

Burial customs

Many of the ornaments and objects which have survived from the Viking period were found by archaeologists in burial grounds. The Norsemen believed the dead had to take their riches with them into the next world, so they were buried with their treasure.

There were many different types of burial. Some were buried in coffins with mounds of earth piled over them, some in graves marked by stones in the shape of a ship and others in the buried ship itself. The body was

This gold shoulder clasp is from a burial ground at Sutton Hoo, England. It dates from before AD 700 but is typical of the treasures found in Viking sites.

sometimes cremated and sometimes not. It is even thought that some people were placed on a ship which was then set alight and floated out to sea. The dead person's horse was sometimes sacrificed and a slave girl was often killed to accompany a noble after death.

Life after death

Brave warriors who died in battle were promised their reward in the halls of the gods after death. Others do not seem to have had much to look forward to. Those who died of sickness or old age went to the Land of the Dead and suffered a gloomy fate (see page 9).

7

NINE WORLDS

The world of the Norse gods was arranged on three levels, one above the other. The whole was made up of nine areas, or worlds. Here you can see the Nine Worlds and the huge World-Tree, **Yggdrasil**, that grew above them and supported them. See how the world began on pages 10-11.

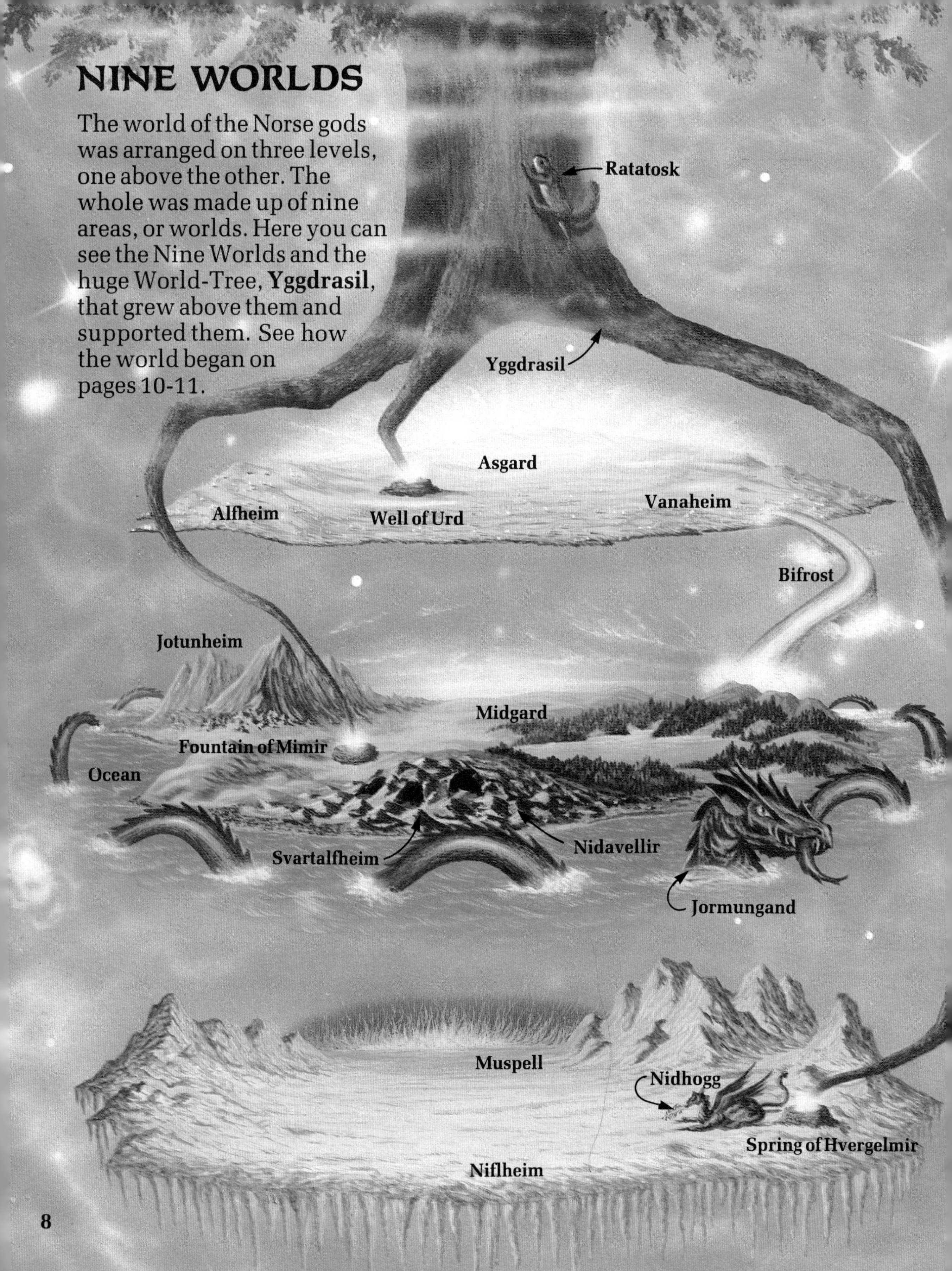

Ratatosk

Yggdrasil

Asgard

Alfheim

Well of Urd

Vanaheim

Bifrost

Jotunheim

Midgard

Fountain of Mimir

Ocean

Svartalfheim

Nidavellir

Jormungand

Muspell

Nidhogg

Spring of Hvergelmir

Niflheim

8

The Nine Worlds of the Norsemen

The Nine Worlds were **Asgard, Vanaheim** and **Alfheim** on the highest level; **Midgard, Jotunheim, Nidavellir** and **Svartalfheim** on the middle level; **Niflheim**, or **Hel** and **Muspell** on the lowest level. You can find out a bit about each of them below.

Yggdrasil

The giant ash-tree, Yggdrasil, towered above the Nine Worlds and held them firmly in place. It had three huge roots. Each root plunged into one of the levels below.

One root went into the **Spring of Hvergelmir** in Niflheim. A vile dragon called **Nidhogg** guarded the spring and gnawed at the root, trying to destroy it.

The second went into the **Fountain of Mimir** in Midgard. The water in this fountain was the source of all wisdom. It was jealously watched by the god, **Mimir** (see pages 22-23).

The third root reached into the **Well of Urd**, in Asgard, which was tended by the **Norns**. There were three Norns. They were very wise old women who tended Yggdrasil. They decided every person's destiny. Even the gods were subject to the fates they decreed.

An eagle and a hawk perched in Yggdrasil's highest branches. Deer nibbled its leaves. The squirrel, **Ratatosk**, ran up and down its trunk, carrying insults between the eagle and Nidhogg.

The leaves of the tree dripped a sweet dew that the bees used to make honey.

Asgard and Vanaheim

On the highest level were the worlds of the gods and goddesses. There were two types of god. The **Aesir** were warrior gods. They lived in Asgard. The **Vanir**, or fertility gods, lived in Vanaheim. Each deity had a magnificent hall of his or her own. A rainbow bridge, called **Bifrost**, connected Asgard to Midgard, below. The watchman of this bridge was the god, **Heimdall**.

Alfheim was also on this level. It was where the **Light Elves** lived.

Midgard

Below Asgard was the Earth, or Midgard. This was the world of humans.

The **Giants** lived on this level, too. Some said their stronghold, **Utgard**, was in the barren mountains of Jotunheim far to the East. Others said that it lay across the vast **Ocean** that surrounded the Earth.

To the north of Midgard was Nidavellir. It was an area of caves and holes belonging to the **Dwarfs**. Nearby was Svartalfheim, where the troublesome **Dark Elves** lived.

Midgard was surrounded by the Ocean. It was so wide that it was thought to be impossible for humans to cross. In the Ocean lurked the terrible World-Serpent, **Jormungand**. He was so big that his body circled Midgard and took his own tail in his mouth. You can read more about him on pages 16-17 and 31.

The Land of the Dead

On the lowest level was Niflheim, the Land of the Dead. It was a gloomy place of ice, snow and eternal darkness. It was ruled by **Hel**, the gruesome Queen of the Dead (see page 17). To reach Niflheim you had to travel for nine days northwards and downwards from Midgard. At the gate waited the ghastly dog, **Garm**, with his bloodstained breast.

The fires of Muspell burned on this level, too. Muspell was guarded by **Surt** and his flaming sword. He was waiting to lead the fiery creatures of Muspell against the gods when the time came for their downfall (see page 38).

THE CREATION

The Norsemen, like all peoples, tried to explain how the world began. Here is what they believed.

Ginnungagap

Before the world existed there was a place of ice and snow in the North, called **Niflheim**. The South was an area of flames and fire named **Muspell**. Between them was a great emptiness known as **Ginnungagap**.

Ymir and Audumla

Eleven rivers flowed out of Niflheim into Ginnungagap where they froze and filled the emptiness. When the ice spread near enough to the heat of Muspell it began to melt. From the melting drops two creatures were formed. One was the first Frost Giant, **Ymir**, and the other was a huge cow, called **Audumla**. Ymir lived by drinking Audumla's milk and the cow licked the salty ice for nourishment.

While Ymir slept he sweated. From his sweat came more Frost Giants.

The birth of the gods

As Audumla was licking the ice one day, a huge, manlike shape began to appear. Within three days she licked the figure free of the ice. This was **Buri**, who in time had a son called **Bor**. Bor married **Bestla**, a Frost Giantess, and they had three sons, **Odin, Vili** and **Ve**. These became the first gods.

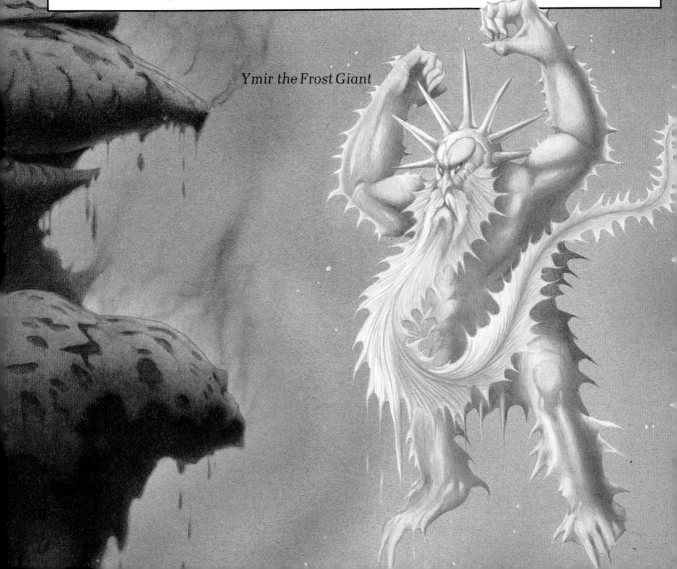

Ymir the Frost Giant

The death of Ymir

Ymir and the Frost Giants were brutal and evil. Odin and his brothers hated them. When they could not stand Ymir any more, they killed him. His blood flowed out in torrents, sweeping away all the Frost Giants except one called **Bergelmir** and his wife, who escaped in a hollow tree-trunk. All the Giants are descended from this pair.

The gods make the world

Odin, Vili and Ve dragged Ymir's body into Ginnungagap and used it to form the world. The Earth was made from his flesh. His bones and teeth became mountains and rocks and his blood filled the rivers and seas. His skull made the dome of the sky and his brains were tossed in the air as clouds.

The gods then took sparks from Muspell and threw them into the sky to be the moon, sun and stars.

The first humans

One day, while walking by the sea, Odin, Vili and Ve found the roots of an ash and an elm tree and made the first humans from them. The ash root became the first man, **Ask**, and the elm root his wife, **Embla**.

The Dwarfs

The gods noticed that maggots had appeared from Ymir's flesh and were crawling about on the Earth. They changed the maggots into small, human-shaped creatures and these became the **Dwarfs**. Four Dwarfs, called **North, South, East** and **West** were given the task of holding up the sky.

Night and Day

Night was a Giant's daughter, and **Day** was her son. Odin gave them both horse-drawn chariots and set them to drive round the world every 24 hours.

The story of Moon and Sun

A human called **Mundulfari** had a son and a daughter who were so beautiful that he called them **Moon** and **Sun** after the planets the gods had made. The gods thought this presumptuous and took the children away. They made Moon drive a chariot drawing the moon while Sun guided the sun's chariot.

Sun followed Moon across the sky. They travelled very fast because both were being chased by great wolves, who would swallow and destroy them if they caught up with them. **Skoll** was the wolf that chased Sun and the beast that pursued Moon was called **Hati**. They were the monstrous children of an ancient Giantess who lived in the Iron Wood on Earth. They eventually played a part in the gods' downfall, as you can see on page 38.

ODIN AND FRIGG

Odin was one of the **Aesir**, or warrior gods. He was the first god to exist, and was father of all the other gods. (His brothers, **Vili** and **Ve**, seem to fade out of Norse Mythology and it is not known what became of them.)

Odin was also King of the gods, both Aesir and **Vanir**. He made the Earth and sky. He created humans and all living creatures (see page 11) and ruled over them.

He was a stern and awesome king. Gods and humans feared his anger, which was not always justified. He could be spiteful and sometimes used his powers in unworthy ways (see the story of **Thor** and the ferryman on page 15). He was respected more than loved and was worshipped by kings and nobles rather than by ordinary people.

God of battle

As the god of battle, Odin caused wars on Earth by flinging down his spear. He decided who won, so warriors did their best to appease him. He was unpredictable, though, and did not always give victory where expected.

God of poetry and wisdom

However, Odin inspired poets as well as warriors. He made a dangerous journey to **Jotunheim** to obtain the Mead of Poetry (see page 33). Sometimes he allowed a human a sip of it and that person became a great poet.

He also sought very hard for wisdom and paid dearly for his knowledge (see page 23). For this reason he was worshipped by seers and magicians.

God of the dead

The bravest of the warriors slain in battle were chosen to join Odin in his great hall, **Valhalla** (see right). He was a god of the dead but he shared this task with others. **Freyja** (see page 20) entertained dead warriors. **Hel** (see pages 9 and 16) took those who died in their beds or of disease.

Valhalla and Valaskjalf

Valhalla, or Hall of the Slain, was Odin's magnificent hall in **Asgard**. Here, he sported and drank with the chosen heroes. They spent their days fighting and were revived every evening to feast and make merry.

Valhalla's walls were made of golden spears and its roof of gold shields. It had 540 doors, each big enough to let 800 armed men through, side by side.

Valaskjalf (meaning Shelf of the Slain) was Odin's other hall where his great throne, **Hlidskjalf**, stood. From his throne, Odin watched over the Nine Worlds. He was helped by two ravens. They flew through the Worlds gathering news which they then whispered in Odin's ears. The ravens were called **Huginn** (Thought) and **Muninn** (Memory).

The Valkyries

The **Valkyries** were female warriors who did Odin's will. They had frightening names like **Shaker**, **Raging Warrior** and **Shrieking**. They swooped over battlefields on horseback, directing the fighting. They picked the heroes to fill Valhalla. A man chosen to die was said to see a Valkyrie just before the fatal blow.

The Valkyries also worked as Odin's servants. They served food and drink to the warriors in Valhalla.

Odin's travels

Odin would often visit the other Worlds in disguise. He travelled in a blue cloak and a broad-brimmed hat which hid his face. On long journeys he rode his wonderful, eight-legged horse, **Sleipnir** (see page 23). His magic spear, called **Gungnir**, and gold arm-ring always accompanied him.

Frigg, queen of the gods

Frigg was Odin's wife and Queen of the gods. She was a Mother goddess and cared for all humans, though she was especially concerned for women and children.

Frigg and Odin had a son, called **Balder**. He died tragically (see page 37) and Frigg mourned him terribly. Because of this, many women felt she would be sympathetic to their sorrows. Their other son, **Bragi**, was married to **Idunn** (see page 25).

Although she was very beautiful and was desired by many men, she was faithful to Odin. She was a match for Odin, though, and could outwit him if she was determined to get her own way.

Like Odin, Frigg could see what the future held for any human and what their fate would be. But she would never tell what she knew.

Odin and Frigg

13

THOR AND SIF

Thor the Thunder-god was **Odin**'s eldest son. His mother was usually said to be **Jorth** (which means Earth). She may have been one of Odin's lovers, or Jorth could simply be a nickname for **Frigg**, who was closely linked with the Earth.

What Thor was like

Thor was an exaggerated, colourful character. He was huge, even for a god, and incredibly strong. He had wild hair and beard and a temper to match. He was never angry for long, though, and easily forgave people.

He did everything on a grand scale – feasting, drinking and fighting. He liked nothing better than a straightforward battle of strength and rarely used tricks or magic like some of the other gods.

Thor the thunder god

His brain did not always match the strength of his body and the other gods sometimes teased him for it. But people like ordinary farmers loved him for his simple outlook. He was probably the most popular of the Norse gods. His symbol was the oak tree.

Thor was called Defender of **Asgard** since he protected it from the gods' enemies. His greatest adversaries were the Giants and there are many tales of his fights with them (on page 28, for example).

God of law and order

Although Thor was a warrior he was also god of law and order, unlike Odin, who stood for war and destruction. As Thor defended Asgard against Giants, so he protected the Norsemen's homes and farms.

Thor was the Keeper of Oaths, too. Copies of his arm-ring were kept in his temples and people swore oaths on them. They were then responsible to Thor to keep their word.

Thor the thunderer

Thor raced across the sky in his chariot drawn by two giant goats, **Toothgnasher** and **Toothgrinder**. It was their hooves that people heard when it thundered on Earth. He controlled the thunder and lightning and brewed up storms by blowing through his beard. Sailors prayed to him for protection from bad weather.

Thor's magic weapons

Thor had a belt which doubled his strength when he buckled it on and iron gauntlets which allowed him to grasp any weapon. You can read about how he got them on page 27. The most famous of Thor's weapons was his hammer, **Mjollnir**. It always hit its target and returned to Thor's hands after use. When a thunderbolt struck Earth, people said that Thor had flung down his hammer. Mjollnir did not only do harm, though. It also had protective powers and people wore small copies of it as jewellery to keep them safe and bring good luck. These charms were used to bless the dead, newborn babies and brides. On page 29, you will see how this tradition helped Thor retrieve his hammer when it was stolen.

Thor and the ferryman

Thor was always more popular than Odin. This story helps to explain why.

Odin was annoyed with Thor. He wanted a magic horse that Thor had. Thor gave it to his son, instead of offering it to Odin (you can read about this on page 28).

Later, Thor was trudging wearily home after a hard fight against the Trolls, when he came to a swollen river. It was too deep to wade. Thor found a ferryman and asked him for a ride.

The ferryman said his name was **Harbard**. He soon proved most unpleasant. He would not take Thor on board and told him that his mother was dead and his wife had run off with a mortal. Then he began to poke fun at the god, who lost his temper and began to shout. He yelled and boasted about his brave deeds but each time the ferryman had a better story.

Thor realized the ferryman did not mean to take him across and stormed off. He had to walk miles to a ford.

Back in Asgard, he found his mother well and his wife faithful as ever. He never discovered that Harbard was Odin in disguise. This was how Odin took out his spite over the horse.

Sif

Thor was married to **Sif**, who was famous for her pure gold, flowing hair. She was a goddess of fruitfulness and plenty. Her hair reminded people of a field of ripe corn and the harvest.

In one of the myths her hair was cut and stolen (see page 26). Her misery until the hair was replaced represented the darkness of the winter season, when the corn did not grow.

Sif and Thor lived in a great hall in Asgard, called **Bilskirnir**, which means Lightning.

BALDER AND TYR

Balder was loved by everyone. He was an **Aesir** god and the son of **Odin** and **Frigg**. He was fair-haired and handsome. His face glowed and he was god of light, purity and beauty. Always gentle and kind, he was also very wise. His good judgement was sought in disputes and he was often able to reconcile enemies. He brought joy and harmony wherever he went.

Balder was happily married to **Nanna** and they lived peacefully in their hall, **Breidablik**, set in tranquil countryside in **Asgard**. They had a son, **Forseti**, who was god of justice.

Tragically, Balder's happiness was not to last. The envy and spite of **Loki** (see opposite) brought about his premature death. You can read the fatal tale and about its terrible consequences on pages 37-38.

Tyr

Tyr was the bravest of the gods. He earned his reputation through his courage in dealing with the monstrous wolf, **Fenrir** (see the story on page 24). One of his hands was torn off by Fenrir's giant jaws and he was often called the One-Handed afterwards.

Tyr was renowned for his honour. He never broke his word so, like **Thor**, he was a god of law and order. His name was used to guarantee contracts, promises and pledges. He was patron of the local gatherings (called the Thing) where Norsemen traditionally passed laws and settled disputes.

Loki's daughter Hel

16

LOKI

Loki had a special place among the gods. His parents were two Fire-Giants, **Farbauti** and **Laufey**, so he was not really a god. But he was the sworn brother and friend of **Odin** and lived with the **Aesir** in **Asgard**.

He was an attractive character – handsome, agile and a great joker. He loved adventures and was exciting to be with. He was nosy, inventive and loved gambling.

These attributes got him into frequent trouble, but he was wily enough to get out of most fixes. He amused the other gods but teased and exasperated them, too. He was very persuasive and the gods often took his advice, which was not always good, and got them into trouble. Only one god, **Heimdall** (see page 18), was always suspicious of Loki.

Loki was especially talented at shape-changing. He could become any animal at will. He often made mischief as a fly (see page

26) and took the form of a mare to get himself out of trouble over a bargain he and the gods made with a stranger (see page 22).

However, as time went on, it gradually became clear to the gods that Loki was not just a handsome joker. He could be cunning, deceitful and unstable. At times he told hurtful stories about others.

Eventually, the gods became wary of his behaviour and began to feel he deserved the trouble he got into when he fooled around with Giants and Dwarfs. They even began to laugh at him and take sides against him. This made Loki bitter and slowly his nature grew darker and more truly evil.

In the end, his spiteful tricks caused the death of **Balder** , which triggered **Ragnarok** or the Doom of the gods (see page 38).

Loki's brood

Odin warned Loki to have nothing to do with the Giantess, **Angrboda**, but Loki defied him and took her as his mistress. They had three monstrous children. They were the wolf, **Fenrir**; the serpent **Jormungand** who was destined to destroy **Thor** (see pages 31 and 38); and a daughter, **Hel**. Hel was grotesque. Her top half was a beautiful woman, but below the waist she was rotting and hideous, like a corpse. She became Queen of the Dead in **Niflheim**. You can read more about Loki's brood on page 24.

Sigyn, Vali and Narvi

Loki's wife was called **Sigyn**. Despite his faults, she loved him and was faithful to him. She stood by him and protected him even after he had caused Balder's death (page 37).

Sigyn and Loki had two sons, **Vali** and **Narvi**, who came to a tragic end after the death of Balder. The gods turned Vali into a wolf and he tore his brother to pieces. They then used Narvi's entrails to bind Loki for his punishment (see page 38).

NJORD, AEGIR AND HEIMDALL

Njord was the most important of the **Vanir** gods, and the chief god of fertility.

Njord was god of the sea and was therefore very important to the seafaring Vikings. He ruled the winds and waves, provided fish for fishermen and favourable winds for traders.

He lived in a hall by the sea. It was called **Noatun**, meaning Shipyard or Anchorage.

Njord married a Giantess called **Skadi**. You can read how this came about on page 25. Skadi was a great huntress and travelled miles on her snow shoes in winter with her bow and arrows.

The marriage was not a success. Skadi loved the mountains and could not bear the sea; Njord could not survive without the smell of the sea and hated the rugged mountains. In the end they lived apart.

Njord was one of the important leaders who swapped places in **Asgard** and **Vanaheim** after the war between the gods (page 22).

Aegir

Aegir and his wife, **Ran,** were also sea gods. They lived on the sea-bed and had nine daughters who moved the waves. Their personalities were changeable, like the sea they lived in. They could be pleasant or violently destructive.

They needed subjects for their kingdom so if a person fell overboard or a ship sank, they would drag the victim to the ocean floor in their nets. There, Aegir and Ran entertained them in their hall, which was crammed with treasure from shipwrecks.

Heimdall

The god **Heimdall** had some very special attributes. He was said to be the son of nine maidens. They may have been the nine daughters of Aegir and Ran . His senses were supernaturally good. He had hearing so acute that he could hear the grass grow and sight so sharp that he could detect movement a hundred miles away. He needed little sleep and was very strong.

Because of his special gifts, he was made watchman of the gods. He guarded **Bifrost**, the rainbow bridge between **Asgard** and **Midgard**. He challenged all strangers and warned the gods of their approach. He had a horn called **Gjall** which he blew in warning. It was kept by the **Fountain of Mimir** (see page 9). Its blast sounded through the Nine Worlds at **Ragnarok**, or the end of the world (see page 38) Heimdall was **Loki's** implacable enemy. They were both fire gods and clashed all the time.

Heimdall rode a gold-maned stallion called **Gulltop**.

Heimdall's journey or the Song of Rig

Once, Heimdall paid a visit to Earth. He disguised himself as a man called **Rig**.

On his journey, he came to a turf hut owned by a poor couple called **Ai** and **Edda** and asked them for food and shelter. Despite being so poor, they shared all they had with him for three nights. As a reward he caused Edda to have a son. The couple called him **Thrall** and he was ancestor to all the serfs in the world. (Serfs were poor farm workers who had no land.)

Rig next came to a comfortable farm owned by **Afi** and his wife, **Amma**. They were prosperous and gladly gave Rig shelter for three days. They were also granted a son for their kindness. He was called **Karl** and all farm-owners were descended from him. Rig moved on until he came to a gracious hall, owned by the noble **Fathir** and his wife **Mothir**. They spared no expense to entertain him for three days. Mothir, too, produced a son who was named **Jarl**.

Jarl grew up handsome and strong. One day he was out hunting when Heimdall appeared. The god taught Jarl some of the wisdom and secret knowledge of the gods. Lastly, he revealed that it was he who had caused Jarl to be born. He told the boy it was his right to go out and win land and treasures. Jarl did as he was told and became a wealthy nobleman. He married **Enna**, a chief's daughter. Their children founded the race of nobles.

Aegir and Ran

FREYJA

The most famous of all the goddesses was **Freyja**. She was a **Vanir**, daughter of the most important Vanir god, **Njord** (see page 18). She had a brother called **Freyr** (see next page). It was said that their mother was Njord's sister.

Goddess of love and beauty

Freyja was goddess of love and beauty. She had been married to the god, **Od**. He had left her and disappeared for some unknown reason. She mourned for him and when she cried she wept golden tears.

Nevertheless, she was very lovely and had many suitors. She took lovers among gods and men but spurned Giants who did not attract her, though they often wooed her.

Her love of beautiful objects sometimes overcame her good sense. Once, she lowered herself to spend the night with four Dwarfs in return for the magnificent necklace, called **Brisingamen**, that they had made.

Goddess of death

As punishment for her bad behaviour over Brisingamen, **Odin** made Freyja a goddess of death. She presided over battles and caused wars between kings on Earth. She flew over the battlefield in her chariot pulled by two cats. She chose half of the bravest warriors to accompany her to **Sessrumnir**, her hall in **Asgard**, after death.

Fertility goddess

Like all the Vanir, Freyja was a fertility goddess. She brought prosperity by granting good harvests and successful fishing. She took special care of women who were getting married or having babies and made sure many healthy children and animals were born.

The boar was her symbol, as it was her brother's. One of Freyja's nicknames was **Syr**, which means sow.

Freyja's magic

After the war between the gods (page 22) Freyja went with her father and brother to live in Asgard with the **Aesir**.

Freyja was a powerful witch and taught the Aesir her skills. She owned a magic falcon skin. When she put it on her spirit could fly through the Nine Worlds.

She made prophecies and foretold the future of all newborn babies.

FREYR

Freyja and Freyr

Freyr was the son of **Njord** (see page 18) and brother to **Freyja** (see previous page).

God of peace and plenty

As a fertility god, like his sister, Freyr granted peace and plenty to his followers. He was not a warrior god, and cared more for giving life than taking it. It was forbidden to carry arms or shed blood on land dedicated to him and outlaws were not allowed in his holy places. His worshippers prayed for his protection in battle, though, and often wore his symbol, the boar, on their helmets.

Freyr's magic possessions

Freyr owned a magic sword that moved through the air of its own accord.

He also possessed the magic ship, **Skidbladnir** (see page 26). It was big enough to hold all the gods but could be folded up and put in his pocket when not in use. It always had a favourable wind.

Freyr's chariot was pulled by a magic, golden boar called **Gullinbursti**, made by the Dwarfs (see page 26). It could run as fast as any mount.

The wooing of Gerd

Freyr was married to the Giantess, **Gerd**. This is the story of their courtship.

One day, Freyr wandered into **Odin**'s hall, **Valaskjalf**, and sat on Odin's throne. He had no right to do this. As he admired the view of the Nine Worlds his eye was drawn to **Jotunheim**, the land of the Giants.

There, leaving her father's hall, was Gerd, a dazzling Frost Giantess. Freyr fell in love on sight. But it was hopeless as he knew he would never be allowed to marry her.

Back in his own hall, Freyr despaired. He could not eat or sleep and bitterly regretted his visit to Valaskjalf. Njord grew worried. He found out what had happened from Freyr's servant, **Skirnir**. Njord was not keen to have a Frost Giantess as a daughter-in-law but could not bear to see his son suffer. So he sent Skirnir to woo Gerd for Freyr. It was too risky to let Freyr go to Jotunheim himself.

Freyr gave Skirnir his magic sword and his magic horse which could see in the dark and gallop through fire. The horse sped to Jotunheim and through the ring of icy fire round Gerd's home.

Gerd received Skirnir coldly. She rejected his offers of love, wealth and eternal youth. Like all of her kind, her heart was ice. Skirnir then tried threats. He laid Freyr's magic sword on the floor, telling Gerd that it would kill her father when he came in.

Afraid, Gerd agreed to meet Freyr. They would meet in nine days' time in the Forest of Barri. Skirnir hurried back in triumph to **Asgard**.

Freyr could hardly bear the wait, but on the ninth day he and Gerd met. Happily, the warmth of his love melted Gerd's frozen heart and she became a warm, loving creature. They returned to Asgard and lived happily there.

21

THE GODS' FIRST EXPLOITS

THE FIRST WAR

The **Vanir** gods originally had magic powers which the **Aesir** did not. **Gullveig** was a Vanir witch. She could predict the future and make gold. One day she visited the Aesir and boasted of her skills, but would not share her secrets. Infuriated, the Aesir killed her and threw her body on a fire.

She rose from the flames unharmed, however. The Aesir tried to kill her twice more but she revived each time. Finally, they were ashamed and left her alone. They gave her a new name, **Heid**, meaning gleaming one.

When the Vanir heard how Gullveig had been mistreated they were very angry. They protested and the argument turned to blows.

In the ensuing fight, the Vanir destroyed **Asgard's** walls and the Aesir did equal damage to **Vanaheim** but neither side could claim a victory so they declared a truce.

The gods decided to swap leaders as a sign of peace. Three of the greatest Vanir – **Njord**, **Freyr** and **Freyja** (see pages 18-21) – joined the Aesir. Only two Aesir went to Vanaheim in return and it was soon clear that they were not of the same quality. These were the warrior, **Honir** and **Mimir**, guardian of the Fountain of Knowledge.

Honir was very brave and Mimir was extremely wise so the Vanir welcomed them at first. But although they worked well together, Honir on his own became confused and could not make intelligent decisions.

The Vanir felt cheated and in revenge they chopped off Mimir's head and sent it back to **Odin**. He preserved it with magic herbs and gave it the power of speech so it could still pass on Mimir's wisdom. He kept it by the Fountain of Knowledge.

Despite these problems, the peace held and the Aesir learned the magic of the Vanir.

REBUILDING ASGARD'S WALL

The **Aesir** were anxious to rebuild **Asgard's** wall. It had been ruined in the war with the **Vanir** (see left). But they could not find anyone to do the job.

Then one day a rider came to Asgard, saying he had a proposal for the gods. He offered to repair the wall. His price was the moon, the sun and **Freyja** as his wife.

The gods (especially Freyja) were outraged but sly **Loki** suggested the gods should accept on condition the work was completed, without help, in six months. They knew this would be impossible, but if the builder agreed, they would get most of the wall mended without paying since the contract would be broken.

The stranger agreed to the terms as long as he could have the help of his horse, **Svadilfari**, which the gods allowed.

The horse dragged huge rocks to the wall in a net and the stranger worked so hard it began to seem he would complete the work in time. The gods were furious and told Loki he must get them out of the bargain.

Loki, the Shape-Changer, had an idea. As the stranger took Svadilfari to fetch a final load of rocks on the last day of the six months, Loki appeared disguised as a beautiful mare and pranced around playfully. Svadilfari ran after the mare into the woods and could not be caught. The workman could not finish the job without him, so he failed.

In his fury, the builder burst out of his magic disguise, revealing his true shape as a Rock-Giant. The gods then had no qualms about killing him for trying to fool them.

Loki wisely stayed away from Asgard for a while. When he returned he brought a fantastic, eight-legged horse, called **Sleipnir**. Sleipnir was the son of Svadilfari and the mare Loki had been. He could gallop over land, sea and air. Loki gave the horse to **Odin** to regain his favour.

Loki on Sleipnir

ODIN'S WISDOM

Odin was hungry for all the wisdom in the world. He began by making a journey and asking questions of everyone he met – Elves, Dwarfs and Giants.

In **Jotunheim** Odin learnt all he could from **Mimir**, guard of the Fountain of Knowledge. Keen to know more, he asked to drink from the Fountain itself. Mimir said he could but that he must pay a high price – one of his eyes. Odin agreed and was one-eyed from then on.

Still Odin wanted to learn more. To do so he paid the final penalty. He became a

sacrificial victim. He hung from a branch of **Yggdrasil** with a spear in his side for nine days and nights. After this ordeal he died. Thus he learnt the wisdom of the dead. By his supernatural powers he came to life again and used what he had learnt for the good of gods and mortals.

Odin brought the Runes from the Land of the Dead. These were magic symbols that warded off danger. Odin taught them to mankind and they carved them in stone to provide magic protection.

23

THE GODS IN DANGER

THE BINDING OF FENRIR

The **Norns** warned the gods that the unnatural children of **Loki** and the evil Giantess, **Angrboda** (see page 17), could bring disaster upon them. So the gods decided to act.

They raided Angrboda's hall and seized her monstrous brood. **Odin** grabbed the serpent **Jormungand** and threw him into the **Ocean**. **Hel** (half-woman, half-corpse) was banished to **Niflheim**. The giant wolf, **Fenrir**, seemed harmless so the gods let him wander free.

These precautions were not enough, though. Jormungand terrorized the seas, Hel became feared as Queen of the Dead and Fenrir grew so fierce that the Norns warned he would cause Odin's death if something was not done.

The gods could not pollute the sacred ground of **Asgard** by simply killing Fenrir, but he had grown so powerful that it was hard to think of a way to restrain him.

Eventually they decided on a trick. They asked Fenrir to test the strength of an iron chain they had made. They tied it round him, hoping he would be unable to break it, but he escaped easily. The gods produced another, stronger chain and tried the same trick, but Fenrir snapped it without effort.

Fenrir

The gods were seriously worried. They sent **Freyr's** servant, **Skirnir**, to the Dwarfs, offering huge rewards for a chain that could bind Fenrir. He returned with what looked like a silken ribbon. The ribbon was magic, however, and was unbreakable.

Once more, they asked Fenrir to test his strength. By now Fenrir was becoming suspicious. When he saw the strange ribbon he refused to be tied in it. The gods promised to free him if the ribbon proved too strong, but Fenrir did not trust them. At last the wolf agreed to the test if one of the gods would put a hand in his mouth as a sign of good faith while he made the attempt. The gods hesitated, then **Tyr** put his hand between Fenrir's teeth.

The wolf was tied up and soon found that however he strained, the bonds got tighter. The gods refused to free him so he clashed his jaws shut and bit off Tyr's hand.

They dragged Fenrir deep underground and tied him to a rock out of harm's way. This was not the end of Angrboda's children, though, as you will find out on page 38.

IDUNN AND THE GOLDEN APPLES

Odin, Loki and **Honir** went exploring on Earth. When they got hungry Loki killed an ox while the others lit a fire. They set the meat to roast but, strangely, it would not cook.

Then the gods heard a voice. It was an eagle in the tree above. He claimed he was preventing the meat from cooking. He would remove his spell if the gods let him eat his fill. The hungry gods agreed and the eagle at once snatched all the best bits.

Loki was enraged and attacked the eagle with a staff. The bird grabbed the staff and flew off with Loki still dangling from it. Loki tried to let go but was held by magic. The eagle deliberately dragged Loki over thorn bushes, glaciers and rocks until he promised he would do anything if the eagle would only let him go.

Loki was made to promise to lure the goddess **Idunn** and her golden apples out of **Asgard** sometime in the next seven days. The golden apples were magic fruit which kept the gods young. Idunn was their keeper.

Loki tricked Idunn into leaving Asgard with her apples. He told her he had found a tree in **Midgard** that bore golden fruit. It might be a new source of the precious apples. He persuaded her to investigate, taking her apples for comparison.

As soon as Idunn set foot in Midgard the eagle swooped down and carried her off to **Jotunheim**. For he was really the Giant **Thiazi** in disguise.

Without the apples, the gods grew old and feeble. They did not know where Idunn was and could not think what to do. **Heimdall** said he had seen Idunn leave Asgard with Loki. They questioned Loki until he told them the truth. They then threatened to kill him unless he brought her back.

Freyja lent Loki her magic falcon skin and he flew to Thiazi's stronghold. He found Idunn a prisoner there. He turned her into a nut so he could carry her in his beak, then fled back to Asgard. Thiazi saw her escape and gave chase in his eagle disguise.

The gods had lit fires to guide Loki and he flew safely over the walls of Asgard. Thiazi plunged after him but in his haste he singed his wings and fell to earth. The gods soon finished him off, despite their weak, aged state. Loki restored Idunn to her proper shape and her golden apples soon revived the gods.

Thiazi's daughter, **Skadi**, came to Asgard seeking compensation for her father's death. The gods offered her one of themselves as a husband but they said she must choose from their feet only. She picked the shapeliest pair, hoping they were **Balder's**. They proved to be **Njord's**, which did not please Skadi (see page 18 for more about their marriage). She was appeased in the end when Odin placed her father's eyes in the sky as stars and gave her the gift of laughter to cheer her up.

25

MAGIC GIFTS FOR THE GODS

TREASURES OF THE GODS

Once when **Thor** was off fighting Giants, **Loki** crept into **Sif's** bedroom and cut off all her wonderful, golden hair.

Thor returned to find Sif heartbroken. He threatened to break every bone in Loki's body unless he replaced her hair.

Loki went to the Dwarfs for help. They made a magic length of hair from spun gold that grew like real hair.

At the same time, they made a magic ship, **Skidbladnir**, and a spear called **Gungnir**. They gave them to Loki for the gods, hoping to win their gratitude.

Loki took the gifts and, on his way home, he visited two more Dwarfs, **Brokk** and **Eitri**. Craftily hoping to get more treasures, he bet his own head that they could not make gifts to equal those he already had.

Challenged, the two Dwarfs forged a golden boar, a gold arm-ring and a war hammer.

Pleased with himself, Loki hurried back to **Asgard**, where he gave Sif her hair. Then he offered **Odin** the arm-ring. He gave **Freyr** the ship and the boar, **Gullinbursti**. He presented the hammer to Thor . It was called **Mjollnir**.

Then Brokk turned up to ask if the gods liked his work. They agreed it was as good as the rest, so he demanded Loki's head in payment of their bet.

What Brokk did not know was that while he had been forging his gifts, Loki had turned into a fly and distracted him just long enough to make him forge Mjollnir's handle slightly too short for perfection. Loki now pointed this out but the gods thought it was a shabby trick and that he deserved to lose his head.

Loki's last chance was a trick with words. He agreed that the Dwarf could have his head, but must not take any of his neck. It was not possible to take one without touching the other, so Loki was saved. Brokk contented

himself with sewing up Loki's mouth to teach him a lesson. The gods laughed at Loki.

Loki went off alone and ripped out the painful stitches. He felt humiliated and resented the gods' laughter. From this time he began to plot his revenge.

The Dwarfs at work

THOR'S MAGIC BELT AND GLOVES

Loki was wearing **Freyja's** falcon skin when the evil Giant, **Geirrod**, caught him. Geirrod and his two foul daughters saw the strange glitter in the bird's eyes and realized it must be a god or magician in disguise.

Loki refused to admit who he was, so Geirrod shut him in a box without food until he gave in. Geirrod said he would be released if he promised to bring **Thor**, unarmed, to the Giant's hall. Loki agreed.

Thor simply enjoyed Loki's company so when he proposed a trip to **Midgard** to meet "two lovely girls", Thor happily went along. Since it was meant to be a pleasure-trip, he left **Mjollnir** at home.

On the way, the gods stayed with the friendly Giantess, **Grid**. Thor mentioned that they were going to meet Geirrod's daughters. Later, when Loki was asleep, Grid explained to Thor that Geirrod was an enemy and was probably plotting something. She gave Thor a belt, which doubled his strength, some iron gauntlets and a magic staff. Loki was worried when he saw Thor's new equipment but dared not say anything.

Next day they came to a river of blood which they tried to wade, but the flow grew deeper and faster. Thor then saw a hideous Giantess who was sending the blood in waves towards them. This was one of Geirrod's daughters. He threw a rock to drive her off but still had to clutch Loki and grab hold of a branch to avoid being swept away.

When they reached Geirrod's hall no one was there so Thor sat down and dozed off. He woke to find his chair being lifted to the ceiling by Geirrod's daughters, who intended to crush him against the roof.

Thor used Grid's staff to push himself away from the beams, then he killed the evil Giantesses. Geirrod himself appeared next, with a ball of red-hot iron held in tongs. He threw it at Thor, who caught it in his iron gloves. He hurled it back with all the strength lent him by Grid's belt. The Giant was killed and Thor returned safely to Asgard. He never really trusted Loki again, though.

THOR AND THE GIANTS

The Giant Hrungnir

THOR'S HEADACHE

One day **Odin** went looking for adventure in **Jotunheim** on his fantastic horse, **Sleipnir**.

The Giant **Hrungnir** saw him coming and was very impressed by Sleipnir. He challenged Odin to a race against his own horse, **Gullfaxi**. Odin accepted.

The horses were a good match and Hrungnir was so busy racing that he did not realize they were heading straight for **Asgard**. They were over the wall into the home of the gods before he knew it.

Hrungnir was sure he had been led into a trap, but Odin seemed friendly and offered him a drink. The gods were scandalized to see a Giant in Asgard. Odin warned them not to harm an unarmed guest.

Hrungnir began to relax and enjoy himself. He drank as much as the **Valkyries** could bring him and became very drunk and rowdy.

Odin began to feel that the Giant was getting out of hand. He sent for **Thor**, who was indignant at Hrungnir's behaviour, and would have dealt swiftly with him. But Hrungnir was quick to point out that it would be cowardly for Thor to kill him as he had no weapon. Thor restrained himself, but arranged to meet Hrungnir in single combat at another time.

The day of the duel came and the enemies faced each other. Thor hurled **Mjollnir** at the Giant. Hrungnir held up a huge whetstone, which he used to sharpen his tools, as a shield.

The hammer shattered the whetstone and one of the sharp, flying chips entered Thor's head. He fell, wounded. But Mjollnir reached its mark, despite the whetstone shield, and Hrungnir was killed. He fell dead on top of Thor. The gods tried to pull Thor from under the Giant but could not shift him.

Thor ordered his servant, **Thialfi**, to go to the Giantess, **Jarnsaxa**. She was an ally of the gods and she and Thor had a son called **Magni**. He was only three years old but already had the combined strength of his parents.

Magni freed Thor easily. Thor was delighted with his son and gave him Hrungnir's horse, Gullfaxi, in thanks. This offended Odin, who had fancied the horse for himself. Odin made Thor pay for this later (see page 15).

From then on, the chip of whetstone in Thor's head gave him terrible headaches.

THE THEFT OF THOR'S HAMMER

Thor woke one morning to find his hammer gone. The worried gods held a council to decide what to do.

Loki offered to find the hammer and **Freyja** lent him her falcon skin so he could fly swiftly in search of it.

He soon discovered that it was **Thrym**, a Frost Giant, who had **Mjollnir**. Thrym said he would return it only if he was sent Freyja as his wife.

Freyja shook with indignation and shed gold tears. This amused Loki who encouraged the gods to send her to Thrym. But **Heimdall**, who disliked Loki, came up with a plan.

Heimdall's plan was that Thor should dress up as a bride and pretend to be Freyja. Once in Thrym's hall he could perhaps recover his hammer. Loki went along to join in the fun, disguised as a bridesmaid.

When Thor and Loki arrived at Thrym's hall the wedding feast was laid. Thor nearly gave himself away by his outrageous appetite, but Loki explained it by saying the "bride" had not eaten for days in her excitement.

Delighted that she was so eager, Thrym called for Mjollnir to bless the bride. He placed the hammer on her knees in the traditional way. At once, Thor grabbed it and threw off his veil. The Giants ran for their lives, though Thor killed Thrym and several others.

29

MORE ADVENTURES OF THOR

THOR'S LESSON IN UTGARD

Thor and **Loki** went to visit **Utgard**. On their way they stayed with a couple so poor that they only had vegetable soup to offer the gods. So Thor killed the goats that pulled his chariot and they had a feast. Thor saved the goats' skins and insisted that all the bones be kept.

The couple's son, **Thialfi**, loved marrow and secretly snapped one of the goats' thighbones to suck. He hid the broken bone under the rest.

Next day, Thor waved his hammer over the skins and bones and brought the goats back to life. But one of them was lame and Thialfi had to confess. Thor took him and his sister, **Roskva**, along as servants in repayment.

One night they discovered a strange hall in the forest. Its door filled the width of one wall. Inside they found a small room off the main hall and slept there. In the night they were woken by a roaring and the ground shook. They were uneasy and left at dawn.

Outside they found the source of the disturbance. It was a Giant snoring. The "hall" was his glove and they had slept in its thumb. The Giant woke and introduced himself as **Skrymir**. He offered to guide them to Utgard and took their food bag to carry. He strode on ahead. When they caught up he was asleep and had sealed the food bag by magic so they could not get anything to eat.

That night Skrymir kept them all awake with his snoring again. Unable to bear it, Thor rose and bashed him over the head with **Mjollnir**. Skrymir went on snoring loudly. Thor hit him three more times but the Giant simply woke complaining that an acorn must have dropped on his head.

Skrymir walked ahead again the next day. He said he would prepare a welcome for them but they found the gates of Utgard closed and had to squeeze through the bars.

At last they reached the hall of the Giant King, **Utgard-Loki**. He laughed at Thor's group and called them puny. He challenged them to beat the Giants at anything.

Loki offered to out-eat anyone. A huge meal was laid and he and the Giant, **Logi**, started to gobble. They met in the middle of the table. Loki ate all his food but Logi chewed bones and dishes, too, so he won.

Thialfi agreed to a race. He ran his fastest but his Giant opponent finished before Thialfi had got half-way.

Thor was sure he could drink more than anyone else. Utgard-Loki gave him a huge drinking horn. He put it to his lips but could not drain it however he gulped.

The Giants then set Thor some easier tasks. First, to lift the King's cat, but he could hardly heave one paw off the ground. Then, to wrestle with an old woman, the King's foster-mother, who got Thor down on one knee.

Humbled and ashamed, Thor let Utgard-Loki show him to the gates of Utgard. There, the King said that now Thor was safely out of Utgard he would confess to tricking him.

Utgard-Loki admitted that Skrymir had been himself in disguise. When Thor had struck him his head had been protected by a magic, invisible hill. He showed Thor the hill and the deep valleys made by his blows.

The Giant whom Loki had challenged was really Fire, which eats everything in its path.

Thialfi had run against Thought, the fastest-moving thing in the world.

Thor's drinking horn had had its tip in the Ocean, which was impossible to drain.

The cat was actually **Jormungand** in disguise, and the old woman was Old Age, who overcomes everyone in the end.

Utgard-Loki warned the gods never to set foot in his kingdom again. Then he and his stronghold vanished. Thor felt a terrible fool, but it had taught him a lesson.

Thor hooks Jormungand

THOR GOES FISHING

The gods ran out of drink so they went to see **Aegir**, who brewed the best ale. He did not have a pot big enough to hold ale for all the gods and asked **Thor** to get him one.

Tyr's mother was married to the Giant, **Hymir**. She would have a suitable cauldron. So Tyr and Thor went to see her. They knew Hymir disliked gods, so they went in disguise.

Tyr's mother welcomed them with a good meal. Hymir was grumpy, especially when Thor polished off two whole oxen. He moaned that now they would have to go hunting.

Next day, Thor and Hymir went fishing. The Giant caught two whales and was pleased with himself. Then Thor cast his line, baited with an ox-head. There was a great thrashing and **Jormungand** himself rose up and snatched the bait. Thor struggled with the serpent and the boat nearly capsized, but he managed to strike it on the head with **Mjollnir**. Stunned, Jormungand sank below the waves. Hymir was impressed.

Then Thor asked to borrow the cauldron. Hymir sulkily said he could if he could smash a certain glass that he produced. Thor flung it at a pillar but the glass was magic and the pillar broke. Tyr's mother told Thor how to break the spell by throwing the glass at Hymir's head. He did so and the glass smashed.

Hymir then had to hand over the cauldron.

31

TALES OF MAGIC AND DISGUISE

OTTAR'S ANCESTORS

Ottar was a handsome young prince who was devoted to **Freyja**. He built shrines and made sacrifices until Freyja had to notice him. When she saw him she fell in love and went to **Midgard** to be with him.

One thing marred their happiness. Ottar had a rival for his throne, called **Angantyr**. To decide which of them should become king without bloodshed they fixed a contest. The one who could correctly recite the longest list of his ancestors would win.

This was no easy task. The only person who knew Ottar's whole family tree was a disagreeable Giantess called **Hyndla**. She also had a magic beer which would enable him to remember all the names.

Freyja wanted to help Ottar. She turned him into her battle-boar, **Hildisvini**, and rode off to see Hyndla. Freyja did not reveal the real reason for her visit but Hyndla guessed it. The Giantess refused to help and took delight in insulting Freyja. With difficulty, Freyja kept her temper and finally persuaded Hyndla to give her the names of Ottar's ancestors.

But however Freyja cajoled, Hyndla refused to give Ottar a sip of the vital memory beer. The goddess lost patience. Tired of being nice, she threw a circle of flame round the Giantess, which drew in closer and closer. Hyndla was afraid and saved herself by giving Ottar a sip of beer, though she cursed it as he drank.

Freyja was not concerned. She could protect Ottar from any curse of Hyndla's.

HOW DENMARK GOT BIGGER

King **Gylfi** of Sweden set out to discover how his subjects were faring. He went travelling in disguise and one night he came across an old beggar-woman. She shared all she had with him – food, fire and blanket. They talked all night and Gylfi learnt a lot from her.

Next morning, Gylfi thanked the woman, then told her who he was. He offered her as much of his kingdom as she could plough with four oxen in a day and a night in return for her kindness.

The old woman was really the goddess **Gefion**. She felt that Gylfi's reward was too generous.

A real beggar-woman would have been overwhelmed to receive so much for so little. Although Gylfi had meant well, she decided to teach him a lesson.

Gefion and her sons

Gefion called her four sons from **Jotunheim**. Their father was a Giant. She was goddess of ploughing and their sons had been born as giant oxen. They went to Sweden and in a day and a night they ploughed a huge chunk of land with their supernatural strength.

They dragged the ploughed land to the coast and floated it over the sea to Denmark. There, they anchored it off the coast and it became the island of Zealand. The hole left in Sweden filled with water and became Lake Malar.

THE MEAD OF POETRY

When the **Aesir** and **Vanir** made peace (see page 22) they all spat into a great jar to seal the treaty. From the divine spittle they shaped a man, called **Kvasir**. He inherited the gods' wisdom and his advice was highly valued.

Two nasty Dwarfs, **Fjalar** and **Galar**, wanted to steal Kvasir's wisdom. They asked him to a feast, then murdered him, catching his blood in two jars and a cauldron. Mixed with honey it made a heady Mead which inspired wisdom and poetry.

These Dwarfs later quarrelled with the Giant, **Gilling**, and killed him. His brother, **Suttung** came looking for him and would have killed the Dwarfs in revenge but they saved their skins by giving him the precious Mead.

Suttung dug a cavern deep in the mountains to store the Mead and set his daughter, **Gunnlod**, to guard it. He boasted about his treasure, though, and soon the gods heard of it and decided that such a precious liquid should belong to them.

Odin disguised himself as a handsome Giant named **Bolverk**. He went to the home of Suttung's brother, **Braugi**, and tricked his servants into killing each other. He then offered to help Braugi, saying he could do the work of nine men all summer. In return he asked for just one sip of the Mead of Poetry. Braugi agreed, though he was not sure Suttung would allow it.

At the end of the summer, Braugi had to admit that he could not keep the bargain. So Bolverk made him tell where the Mead was kept and bore a hole into the cavern with his magic auger, or drill. Odin at once turned into a snake and wriggled down the hole.

In the cavern, Odin became Bolverk again. He paid court to Gunnlod, who fell in love with him. Soon, he persuaded her to give him a sip of Mead. When she brought him the jars, he quickly drained all three. He held the Mead in his mouth and turned himself into an eagle to fly back to **Asgard**. And that was how the gods got the Mead of Poetry.

THE CURSE OF THE RING

ANDVARI'S GOLD

Odin, Loki and **Honir** were once again in **Midgard**, dressed as ordinary men. By a river they watched an otter catch a salmon. Loki killed the otter for its fine skin and they had the salmon for supper.

They asked for shelter that night at a nearby farm. The farmer, **Hreidmar**, was strangely unwelcoming but the gods put it down to bad manners and soon fell asleep.

In the night, Hreidmar and his sons, **Regin** and **Fafnir**, seized their guests and tied them up. Odin demanded an explanation and Hreidmar revealed that he was a magician. Each day he turned one of his sons into an otter to go fishing. The strangers had killed him.

The gods were shocked and offered to compensate. The farmer asked for enough gold to stuff the otter skin and make a pile over it when held upright.

Loki was freed to fetch the gold. He dived to the sea-bed to borrow **Ran's** net which caught whatever it was cast at. Then he sought out a pool deep in the caves of **Svartalfheim**. He cast the net and caught a huge pike which immediately resumed its real shape as **Andvari**, a Dwarf.

Andvari was famous for his hoard of gold. Loki threatened to strangle him unless he handed it all over. The Dwarf had no choice and led Loki to his secret store.

Loki's sack was full and he was about to leave when he spotted a gold ring on Andvari's finger. Andvari begged Loki not to take it, but he insisted. Dancing with rage, Andvari placed a curse on the gold to bring misery to whoever owned it. The ring he cursed to destroy its wearer.

When Loki returned, Odin and Honir were freed. The otter skin was stuffed with gold and held up by the tail. Gold was piled over it until it was hidden except for one whisker.

Hreidmar demanded Andvari's gold ring, which Loki had kept, to finish the job. Loki warned him of the curse, but he did not care.

Before long, the curse began to work. Greedy for the gold, Fafnir murdered his father. Regin claimed his half of the treasure but Fafnir ran off with the lot. Using the skills learnt from his father, Fafnir turned himself into a dragon and jealously guarded his trove.

Regin wandered far away but he brooded on revenge and eventually found a way to destroy Fafnir (see below).

THE CURSE IS FULFILLED

Many stories are told of how the curse on **Andvari's** gold ended. This is probably the best-known.

After **Fafnir** killed his father to get **Andvari's** gold (see above), his sister, **Hjordis,** married **Sigmund**. Sigmund died before their son, **Sigurd**, was born. Fafnir's brother, **Regin**, cared for his nephew.

Regin taught Sigurd that it was his duty to avenge his grandfather and kill Fafnir, who had become a dragon to guard his trove.

Sigurd grew up strong and brave and slew the dragon. He roasted and ate its heart, whose magic enabled him to talk to the birds.

The gold was now Regin's but he could not bear to share it, even with Sigurd, so he plotted to kill him. The birds warned Sigurd who killed Regin to save himself. He then inherited the gold.

Meanwhile, the **Valkyrie Brynhild** was in trouble. She sometimes became a swan, flew to Earth and removed her disguise to go swimming. One day, a man stole her feathers and would not return them until she had changed the course of a battle.

Brynhild's meddling brought defeat to one of **Odin's** favourites. As punishment, Odin put her into a magic sleep in a castle ringed by fire.

She would only wake if someone braved the flames. Even so, she would no longer be a Valkyrie but a human.

It was Sigurd, seeking the chance to prove his courage, who rescued Brynhild. They fell in love and planned to marry. Before the wedding could take place, Sigurd visited King **Giuki** and Queen **Grimhild** of the Nibelungs. Wicked Grimhild knew of Sigurd's gold and wanted it. She gave him a love potion so he fell in love with and married her daughter, **Gudrun**, forgetting Brynhild.

Gudrun's brother, **Gunnar**, wanted to marry Brynhild. Indifferent now, Sigurd wooed her for him. Brynhild married Gunnar but was so hurt and jealous that she arranged Sigurd's murder, then killed herself.

The curse continued. The gold now belonged entirely to the Nibelungs. Gudrun re-married and made her husband, **Alti**, kill Sigurd's murderer. Then Alti killed Gudrun's brothers so she caused his death in revenge. Gudrun herself and her sons all died violently before the curse faded.

The guardian of the gold

35

AGNAR AND GEIRROD

The King of the Goths had two sons called **Agnar** and **Geirrod**. When Agnar was ten and Geirrod eight they took a boat to go fishing, despite warnings never to go out alone.

A storm arose and the boys were driven far out to sea. By next morning they were near an unknown shore. The nearest shelter was a poor hut, where they were welcomed by an old peasant couple. As the winter weather had closed in, the boys could not go home and stayed there during the cold months.

The peasants treated them kindly. The old man liked Geirrod best, while his wife favoured Agnar. They both taught the boys many things. When spring came they put them in a boat and sent them home.

The peasants were actually **Odin** and **Frigg** in disguise. Geirrod was really a horrid boy, although Odin preferred him. As the brothers neared their home shore, Geirrod grabbed the oars, jumped overboard and pushed the boat back out to sea, leaving Agnar adrift.

Geirrod went home and told his father that Agnar had drowned. The king was overjoyed to see his younger son. He named Geirrod his heir and in time he became king.

Agnar survived but led a wild life. Geirrod grew up even worse and was a very bad king. He was cruel and greedy for gold.

Odin and Frigg watched their foster-sons with interest. Odin teased Frigg about Agnar's wild ways, but would not hear a word against Geirrod. Frigg was annoyed and dared Odin to go to Geirrod's court in disguise to see for himself how guests were treated.

Frigg sent her maid, **Fulla**, to warn Geirrod against a magician who might come to his court. Geirrod would know him because the dogs would not bark at him.

Soon a stranger in a blue cloak and large hat appeared at court. The fierce dogs ignored him and Geirrod thought this must be the very magician. The visitor gave his name as **Grimnir**, but instead of being welcomed he was tied to a spit between two fires.

Only Geirrod's son, called **Agnar** after his lost uncle, took pity on Grimnir. He brought him a horn of ale to ease his suffering. Suddenly, Odin threw off his disguise and broke his bonds. Terrified, Geirrod tried to attack him but fell on his own sword and was killed. Odin vanished, but watched over young Agnar when he became king as a reward for his kindness.

THE DEATH OF BALDER

Balder, the gentlest god, began to have nightmares about death. He told **Odin** and **Frigg**, but neither they nor the other gods could explain it.

Odin galloped to **Niflheim** on **Sleipnir**. In **Hel's** hall he sought out the ghost of a great seeress. She said Balder was doomed and that Odin could not prevent it.

Frigg would not accept Balder's fate. She made a list of every harmful thing, then went through the Nine Worlds making them swear never to hurt Balder. Fire, water, stones, metals, plants and birds and diseases all swore. Frigg felt happier, believing nothing could now kill her son.

The gods found a new game. They threw things at Balder just to see them turn safely aside. Only **Loki** was not happy. He was jealous of Balder. Disguised as an old woman, he questioned Frigg. She admitted that one plant had not made the promise – an insignificant sprig of mistletoe.

Full of hatred, Loki found the plant and made a dart from it. He joined the gods in their latest game and asked Balder's blind brother, **Hod**, if he would like to play. Hod was delighted. Loki gave him the mistletoe dart and guided his aim. It pierced Balder's heart and he fell dead.

Frigg begged someone to go to Niflheim and offer Hel any ransom she asked to release Balder from death. **Hermod**, one of Odin's sons, volunteered.

Balder's body was given a hero's burial. It was placed on his ship, which was piled with treasure and set alight. The Giantess **Hyrrokin** pushed it out to sea. Balder's wife, **Nanna**, died of a broken heart and was buried with him.

In Niflheim, Hermod told Hel why he had come. She said that if Balder was so well-loved, everyone and everything in the Nine Worlds would weep for him. If they did, she would let him return to **Asgard**.

Hermod hurried back with this news and the gods at once went to every corner of the Nine Worlds, asking everyone and everything to cry for Balder. But there was one evil Giantess who would not weep. No amount of pleading would make her shed a tear, so Balder had to stay in the Land of the Dead. The Giantess was actually Loki in disguise. He smiled at what he had done.

Hyrrokin with Balder's funeral ship

THE END OF THE WORLD

LOKI'S PUNISHMENT

Loki avoided the gods after **Balder's** death. The gods mourned bitterly, but eventually decided the mourning must end. So **Aegir** and **Ran** held a feast. **Thor** was away fighting Trolls and Loki was not invited but everyone else was there.

In the middle of the banquet, Loki appeared. Goaded by the sight of the gods' happiness, he began to mock them each in turn. He pointed out their weaknesses and told their secrets.

At this moment Thor came in. Loki threw insults at him, too, then fled. The gods had had enough. They set off to hunt Loki, who became a salmon and leapt into a waterfall to escape. The gods knew his tricks by now and were not fooled. They caught him in a net, which was fitting as Loki had invented the net when Ran was looking for something to catch fish in.

The gods decided that death was too easy for Loki and that he ought to suffer. They turned his son **Vali** into a wolf and let him tear his brother **Narvi** to pieces. They tied Loki across sharp rocks in a cave deep in the mountains.

Skadi placed a great snake among the stalactites hanging from the roof. It dripped venom from its fangs onto Loki's face, causing him agony. The gods felt that this torture was just, but took no joy in their revenge.

Loki's loving wife **Sigyn** sat by her husband. Whatever he had done, she forgave him. She held a bowl to catch the poison and spare Loki's pain. But now and then she had to empty the bowl and the fiery poison struck Loki once more. He writhed in agony until the Earth shook.

Loki's wickedness and **Balder's** death herald the coming of the end of the world. This is to be the Doom of the gods, called **Ragnarok**, and is still to come.

RAGNAROK

According to predictions, quarrels between gods and Giants will become fiercer and more frequent at this time. There will be constant war on Earth and men will slay their own fathers and brothers. **Midgard** will freeze, killing all humans, except one pair who will climb into **Yggdrasil's** branches for refuge.

Garm and Tyr

The dreadful wolves, **Skoll** and **Hati** (see page 11), will finally catch and swallow the sun and moon. The stars will go out, leaving the world in darkness.

Loki and **Fenrir** will break their chains and join sides against the gods. **Jormungand** will heave himself out of the waves and invade the land, making the Earth shudder.

Loki will lead an attack on **Asgard**. The Giants and the fiery beings from **Muspell** will join him. **Hel** will bring her dead souls to fight on his side with **Garm** and all evil creatures.

Heimdall's horn, **Gjall**, will sound a warning through the Nine Worlds. The field of battle has already been chosen. It is a vast plain, called **Vigard**, and there the gods will face their enemies and they will destroy each other.

Fenrir will kill **Odin** and then be killed by Odin's son, **Vidar**; Loki and Heimdall will slay each other; **Thor** will destroy Jormungand, only to die from the serpent's venom; Garm and **Tyr** will die fighting each other and thousands more will perish in the gruesome battle.

Surt (see page 9) will fling fire in all directions and destroy Asgard and Midgard. The Earth will sink into the sea and all life vanish. That is Ragnarok, the end of the world.

A NEW START

All hope for the future does not end at **Ragnarok**, however. Although the Nine Worlds will be destroyed, **Yggdrasil** will survive. Land will rise again from the **Ocean** and a fresh, green Earth will emerge. **Lif** and **Lifthrasir**, the couple who hid in Yggdrasil, will climb down and renew the human race.

Before the sun is swallowed by **Skoll**, she will have a daughter who will return after Ragnarok to light the new world. Plants and animals will gradually reappear.

There will be survivors among the gods, too. Odin's sons, **Vidar** and **Vali** are expected to remain alive. **Thor's** sons, **Modi** and **Magni** are destined to find **Mjollnir** and carry on. **Balder**, **Nanna**, **Hod** and **Honir** will revive and start a new race of gods who will live in peace.

WHO'S WHO

This section is a Who's Who of characters and creatures in the Norse Myths. Any character, place or object whose name appears in bold type in this book has an entry here. Places and Things are in their own sections on page 47.

The Who's Who tells you about the family, doings, personality, appearance and magic powers of each character. It is arranged alphabetically and some abbreviations have been used to save space. You can find out how to understand the entries in the example below.

Entry name, which you look up.

Category: Type of creature.

Distinguishing Features: Special or unusual physical appearance.

Supernatural Attributes: Magical powers or protection.

Abbreviations:
s.=son   lo.=lover
d.=daughter   v.=very
grands.=grandson esp.=especially
m.=married   incl.=including

Pronounciation guide. In this guide ss = hard s as in "sit"; gh = hard g as in "go"; ow is as in "fowl"; a on its own is as in "day". You always emphasize the first syllable.

AUDUMLA (ow-doom-la) "Nourisher". *Category:* supernatural animal. *Family Status:* emerged from nothingness at beginning of world. *Career:* existed in Ginnungagap; nourished first Frost Giant, Ymir, with her milk; licked Bor, father of the gods, out of primeval ice. *Personality:* maternal; passive. *Distinguishing Features:* a giant cow. *Supernatural Attributes:* neverending supply of nourishing milk. **Page 8.**

Associations (if any): Things linked with the character.

Meaning of name.

Family Status: Names of husbands/wives/lovers/children.

Career: Famous deeds and role played in the myths.

Personality: Personality traits from clues in the myths.

Page numbers of main references in this book.

AEGIR (a-gear). *Category:* Vanir god. *Family Status:* m. Ran; nine daughters. *Career:* god of the sea; made his fortune with treasure from shipwrecks; gathers drowning victims in net and entertains them in his underwater hall; brewer to the gods. *Personality:* unpredictable; calm at times; stormy moods. *Distinguishing Features:* lives underwater. *Supernatural Attributes:* controls the waves through his nine daughters; directs the winds. **Page 18, 31, 38.**

AESIR (a-seer). *Category:* gods. *Family Status:* s. and d. of Odin. *Career:* warriors; Keepers of the Dead; judges of human behaviour; main leaders – Odin, Thor, Balder, Tyr, Frigg, Sif. *Personality:* varied. *Supernatural Attributes:* superhuman strength and courage; shape-changing ability; possess many magic weapons and animals. **Page 6, 9, 22, 23.**

AFI (ah-fee) "Grandfather". *Category:* human. *Family Status:* m. Amma; one s. Karl, given by Heimdall. *Career:* farmer; small landowner; chosen by gods to be ancestor of all farm-owners. *Personality:* hardworking; generous; worthy. **Page 19.**

AGNAR (ag-nar).i. *Category:* human. *Family Status:* s. of King of the Goths. *Career:* heir to throne of the Goths; shipwrecked with brother, Geirrod, when ten years old; cared for by Odin and Frigg in disguise; favourite of Frigg; set adrift and abandoned by Geirrod at end of their journey home; survived but led wild life;

became smith to King Hjalprek of Jutland. *Personality:* adventurous; fond of bad company, wild women, drinking etc. **Page 36.**

AGNAR (ag-nar).ii. *Category:* human. *Family Status:* s. of Geirrod. *Career:* pitied Odin when he was tied to a spit in Geirrod's court and gave him a drink; inherited throne of the Goths. *Personality:* kind-hearted. *Supernatural Attributes:* enjoyed protection of Odin for his act of kindness. **Page 36.**

AI (ah-ee) "Great Grandfather". *Category:* human. *Family Status:* m. Edda; one s. Thrall, granted them by Heimdall. *Career:* poor labourer; given by gods to be ancestor to all labourers. *Personality:* humble; generous. **Page 19.**

ALTI (al-tee). *Category:* human. *Family Status:* m. Gudrun; several sons. *Career:* Gudrun's second husband; avenged death of her first husband, Sigurd, by killing his murderer; became greedy for gold Gudrun's family had and murdered Gudrun's brothers for it; was despatched by Gudrun in revenge. *Personality:* weak; easily dominated; avaricious. *Associations:* linked to the real character, Attila the Hun. **Page 35.**

AMMA (am-ah) "Grandmother". *Category:* human. *Family Status:* m. Afi; one s. Karl, granted to them by Heimdall. *Career:* farmer's wife; chosen by gods to raise ancestor of all farm-owners. *Personality:* maternal; generous. **Page 19.**

ANDVARI (and-varri). *Category:* Dwarf. *Career:* gold-collector; keeper of magic ring; forced to give all his treasure to Loki to pay ransom for death of Hreidmar's son; cursed gold and ring when taken from him. *Personality:* greedy; solitary; vindictive. *Distinguishing Features:* took form of a pike and lived in dark pool in Svartalfheim. *Supernatural Attributes:* shape-changing ability; cursing and spell-casting. **Page 34, 35.**

ANGANTYR (an-gan-tier). *Category:* human. *Career:* pretender to Ottar's throne; entered contest with Ottar that each should recite correctly a list of his ancestors; lost contest and throne. *Personality:* ambitious. **Page 32.**

ANGRBODA (anger-bodda) "Distress-Bringer". *Category:* Giantess. *Family Status:* lo. of Loki; three children, Fenrir, Hel, Jormungand. *Career:* enemy of the gods; had much disapproved-of affair with Loki; produced monstrous children she could not control. *Personality:* evil. *Distinguishing Features:* giant size. *Supernatural Attributes:* giving birth to monsters. **Page 17, 24.**

ASK (assk) "Ash". *Category:* human. *Family Status:* m. Embla; many children. *Career:* created from ash branch found on beach by Odin; given life; first human. *Personality:* simple; obedient. *Distinguishing Features:* mortal. **Page 11.**

AUDUMLA (ow-doom-la) "Nourisher". *Category:* supernatural animal. *Family*

Status: emerged from nothingness at beginning of world. **Career:** existed in Ginnungagap; nourished first Frost Giant, Ymir, with her milk; licked Bor, father of the gods, out of primeval ice. **Personality:** maternal; passive. **Distinguishing Features:** a giant cow. **Supernatural Attributes:** neverending supply of nourishing milk. **Page 10.**

BALDER (bal-der). **Category:** Aesir god. **Family Status:** s. of Odin and Frigg; m. Nanna; one s. Forseti. **Career:** giving advice; reconciling enemies; called Bright One; hated by Loki for his popularity; developed morbid fancies about death; Frigg made everything in the world swear not to harm him (except mistletoe, which she missed); dreams of death realized when Loki gave mistletoe dart to Hod to throw at him; his death heralded Ragnarok, the Doom of the gods. **Personality:** wise; gentle; beloved. **Distinguishing Features:** fair hair; shining face. **Supernatural Attributes:** immunity to all harmful things, except mistletoe. **Page 16, 25, 37, 39.**

BERGELMIR (bare-ghel-mere). **Category:** Giant. **Family Status:** father to all Giants. **Career:** escaped drowning in Ymir's blood when Ymir killed by Odin; rode away in hollow tree-trunk with wife; replenished Giant population. **Personality:** strong survival instinct. **Distinguishing Features:** enormous proportions. **Page 11.**

BESTLA (best-lah). **Category:** Giantess. **Family Status:** d. of Ymir; m. Bor; three s. Odin, Vili, Ve. **Career:** Frost Giantess; mother to the first gods. **Page 10.**

BOLVERK (boll-verk). **Category:** god/Giant. **Family Status:** Odin in disguise. **Career:** Odin became Bolverk to obtain Mead of Poetry; tricked the Giant Braugi's servants into killing each other; helped Braugi in the fields then forced him to tell where his brother kept the Mead of Poetry in payment; wooed Giantess Gunnlod who was guarding the Mead; persuaded her to give him a sip, then sucked it all into his mouth and flew off in form of an eagle. **Personality:** charming; persuasive; fatally attractive to Giantesses. **Distinguishing Features:** giant size; v. handsome. **Supernatural Attributes:** shape-changing ability. **Page 33.**

BOR (bore). **Category:** supernatural being. **Family Status:** s. of Buri, who was licked from the original ice by Audumla, the giant cow; m. Bor; three s. Odin, Vili, Ve. **Career:** father of the gods. **Page 10.**

BRAGI (bra-ghee). **Category:** god. **Family Status:** s. of Odin and Frigg; m. Idunn. **Career:** god of poetry, eloquence and wisdom; greets new arrivals in Valhalla and sings songs celebrating their deeds. **Personality:** intellectual; poetic. **Supernatural Attributes:** inspiring humans to poetry. **Page 13.**

BRAUGI (brow-ghee). **Category:** Giant. **Family Status:** brother to Gilling and Suttung. **Career:** used by Odin to get at the Mead of Poetry; Odin, in disguise as Giant, Bolverk, killed all his servants,

then offered to work for him in return for sip of Mead owned by Suttung; agreed to bargain, but could not keep it as Suttung would not give Bolverk any Mead; forced to reveal where Mead was hidden and Odin stole it. **Personality:** gullible. **Distinguishing Features:** v. big. **Page 33.**

BROKK (brock). **Category:** Dwarf. **Career:** superb smith and jeweller; maker (with Eitri) of golden boar Gullinbursti, Odin's gold arm-ring and Thor's hammer Mjollnir; made wager of Loki's head that his work was as good as any other Dwarf's; gods agreed but Brokk was denied his prize when Loki said he could take the head but must not cut off any of his neck; this was impossible; sewed up Loki's mouth in revenge. **Personality:** aggressive; proud of his skill; somewhat bragging. **Distinguishing Features:** small; unattractive and blackened from the smithy. **Page 26.**

BRYNHILD (brin-hild). **Category:** supernatural being/human. **Family Status:** servant to Odin; lo. of Sigurd; m. Gunnar. **Career:** Valkyrie; liked to visit Earth in swan disguise to swim; had swan feathers stolen by a man who made her change the course of a battle before he would return them; this caused a favourite of Odin's to lose battle; stripped of Valkyrie status; placed in magic sleep in castle surrounded by fire; rescued by and was to marry Sigurd; became victim of curse of Andvari's gold, which Sigurd owned; cheated of happiness by evil plans of Queen Grimhild, who wanted the gold; Sigurd married Grimhild's d. Gudrun instead of her; Brynhild forced to marry Gunnar; in desperation, arranged Sigurd's death; committed suicide. **Personality:** unlucky; tragic figure; latterly, bitter and vengeful. **Distinguishing Features:** great warrior as a Valkyrie; v. beautiful. **Associations:** she was called Brunnhilde in Richard Wagner's opera version of the story of Sigurd and the ring, called "Der Ring des Nibelungen". **Page 35.**

BURI (boo-ree). **Category:** supernatural being. **Family Status:** licked from the primeval ice by the giant cow, Audumla; produced one s. Bor. **Career:** grandfather to the first gods. **Page 10.**

DARK ELVES. See **ELVES.**

DAY. Category: Giant. **Family Status:** s. of Night. **Career:** followed his mother in horse-drawn chariot, encircling the world once every 24 hours. **Personality:** reliable. **Distinguishing Features:** brought light. **Page 11.**

DWARFS. Category: supernatural beings. **Family Status:** created by gods from maggots crawling in the flesh of Ymir. **Career:** usually skilled craftsmen; hoarding gold and precious jewels; trying to win favour

of the gods; attempting to woo goddesses; usually enemies of Giants. **Personality:** greedy; cunning; sometimes downright evil. **Distinguishing Features:** small stature; ugly features; sometimes physical deformity. **Page 7, 11, 26, 34.**

EAST. Category: Dwarf. **Career:** holding up one corner of the sky with North, South and West. **Page 11.**

EDDA (edda) "Great Grandmother". **Category:** human. **Family Status:** m. Ai; one s. Thrall, granted them by Heimdall. **Career:** poor labourer's wife; chosen to bring up the ancestor of all farm labourers. **Personality:** humble. **Page 19.**

EITRI (a-tree). **Category:** Dwarf. **Career:** metal-worker/smith; helped Brokk make the hammer Mjollnir, gold boar Gullinbursti and gold arm-ring. **Page 26.**

ELVES. Category: supernatural beings. **Career:** can be Light or Dark; Light Elves live in Alfheim and are good, helpful; Dark Elves live in caves and holes of Svartalfheim and are mischievous trouble-makers. **Distinguishing Features:** small; human-shaped. **Page 2, 7, 9.**

EMBLA (em-bla) "Elm". **Category:** human. **Family Status:** m. Ask; many children. **Career:** first human woman; created by Odin from elm branch found on beach; given life; populated Earth with humans. **Personality:** simple, obedient. **Distinguishing Features:** mortal. **Page 11**

ENNA (en-ah). **Category:** human. **Family Status:** m. Jarl; many children. **Career:** chieftain's daughter; married and became ancestor to the noble classes. **Personality:** dignified. **Page 19.**

FAFNIR (fahf-near). **Category:** human. **Family Status:** s. of Hreidmar. **Career:** farmer; visited by Odin, Loki and Honir in disguise; gods accidentally killed his brother (disguised as an otter); Fafnir, his father and brother Regin bound the gods while they slept and demanded compensation; Loki got them gold from Andvari the Dwarf; Andvari cursed the gold, esp. a gold ring; driven by the curse, Fafnir killed his father to get the gold; refused to share it with Regin; ran away and turned himself into a dragon to guard treasure; killed by his nephew, Sigurd, on instigation of Regin. **Personality:** unremarkable until affected by curse; then greedy; ruthless; selfish. **Distinguishing Features:** became a dragon. **Supernatural Attributes:** wizardry, learnt from his father; shape-changing. **Page 34.**

FARBAUTI (far-bowt-ee) "Cruel Striker". **Category:** Giant. **Family Status:** one s. Loki. **Distinguishing Features:** immense size. **Page 17.**

FATHIR (fath-ear) "Father". **Category:** human. **Family Status:** m. Mothir; one s. Jarl, given to them by Heimdall. **Career:** rich landowner; chosen by gods to raise the ancestor of all nobles. **Personality:** generous; noble. **Page 19.**

FENRIR (fen-rear). *Category:* monster. *Family Status:* s. of Loki and Giantess Angrboda. *Career:* enemy of the gods; allowed to roam free by the gods, even after his brother and sister (Jormungand and Hel) were banished; grew huge and violent until he was a threat to the gods; gods tricked him into testing his strength on a magic rope made by Dwarfs; bound by the rope and could not break free; bit off Tyr's hand, which had been placed in his mouth as assurance against trickery; was kept prisoner underground; future role to break free at Ragnarok and kill Odin; destined to be killed by Odin's son, Vidar. *Personality:* vicious; malicious trouble-maker. *Distinguishing Features:* a huge, fierce wolf. *Supernatural Attributes:* incredible strength. **Page 17, 24.**

FJALAR (fyah-lar). *Category:* Dwarf. *Family Status:* brother of Galar. *Career:* craftsman; perpetrator of evil deeds with his brother; murdered Kvasir and made Mead of Poetry from his blood; drowned the Giant Gilling and killed his wife; saved his own skin by giving the Mead to Gilling's brother, Suttung, when he came for revenge. *Personality:* heartless; treacherous; self-seeking. *Distinguishing Features:* small; ugly. **Page 33.**

FORSETI (force-ett-ee). *Category:* god. *Family Status:* s. of Balder and Nanna. *Career:* god of justice; arbitrator in quarrels. *Personality:* high moral standards; good judgement; fair. **Page 16.**

FREYJA (fray-ah). *Category:* Vanir goddess. *Family Status:* d. of Njord; sister of Freyr; m. Od. *Career:* fertility goddess; goddess of love and beauty; abandoned by Od and mourned him permanently; moved to Asgard as part of pact to end war between gods; taught magic to the Aesir; very fond of gold and jewels; took many lovers; bothered by unwanted attentions of Giants and Dwarfs; became goddess of the Dead as punishment for lowering herself to spending the night with four Dwarfs to obtain the necklace, Brisingamen, that they had made; surveyed battlefields and chose warriors to be entertained in her hall, Sessrumnir; often teased by Loki; fell in love with a human, Ottar; lived with him on Earth and helped him secure his throne by magic; often called Syr, meaning sow, her emblem. *Personality:* proud; judgement affected by desire for beautiful objects. *Distinguishing Features:* cries golden tears. *Supernatural Attributes:* magic powers; can fly when her spirit puts on falcon skin she possesses; drives chariot drawn by two cats, which fly through the air. **Page 20, 22, 25, 27, 32.**

FREYR (fray-er). *Category:* Vanir god. *Family Status:* s. of Njord; brother to Freyja. m. Gerd. *Career:* god of fertility and plenty; protected warriors in battle; moved to Asgard with Njord and Freyja in pact to end war between the gods; paid for his disobedience in sitting on Odin's throne to survey the Nine Worlds, which was forbidden, when he saw and fell in love with Giantess, Gerd; suffered horribly for love until Njord helped him woo Gerd and eventually marry her; will die at Ragnarok because he gives away his magic sword to Skirnir. *Personality:* bold; inquisitive; non-violent. *Supernatural Attributes:* owns golden boar, Gullinbursti; has magic ship, Skidbladnir; uses sword that can move through the air of its own accord. **Page 21, 26.**

FRIGG (frig). *Category:* Aesir goddess. *Family Status:* m. Odin; two s. Balder, Bragi. *Career:* Queen of the gods; Mother goddess; mourns death of Balder; helps women in labour; likes to visit Earth in disguise and intervene in human lives; holds her own with Odin – taught him a lesson when they argued over which of their two foster-sons, Agnar and Geirrod, had turned out worse. *Personality:* regal; independent; clever. *Supernatural Attributes:* shape-changing. *Associations:* the English word Friday comes from "Frigg's day". **Page 13, 14, 37.**

FULLA (full-ah). *Category:* goddess. *Career:* maidservant to Frigg; sent to warn King Geirrod of the approach of a magician, who is really Odin in disguise. *Personality:* willing; obedient. **Page 36.**

GALAR (gay-lar). See **FJALAR**.

GARM (garm). *Category:* monster. *Career:* guardian of the gates of Hel; seeing off unwanted visitors; will lead the dead out of Hel to fight the gods at Ragnarok; he will rip Tyr's throat out and be killed by the god at the same time. *Personality:* ferocious; unthinkingly violent; evil. *Distinguishing Features:* a huge hound with a blood-stained breast. **Page 9, 39.**

GEFION (ghev-yon). *Category:* goddess. *Family Status:* lo. of a Giant; four s. giant oxen. *Career:* goddess of ploughing; famous for teaching King Gylfi a lesson; was in disguise as an old woman and shared her food and fire with him; he offered her as much of the kingdom of Sweden as she could plough with four oxen in one day in thanks; she got her sons to plough a huge area and towed it away to Denmark, where it formed the island of Zealand. *Personality:* moral; sensitive to feelings of others. **Page 32-33.**

GEIRROD (gay-rod).i. *Category:* human. *Family Status:* s. of King of the Goths; one s. Agnar. *Career:* shipwrecked with his brother, Agnar, when eight years old; cared for by Odin and Frigg in disguise; became Odin's favourite; jumped overboard, taking oars and abandoning Agnar to drift in the boat in which they returned home; went home, claimed Agnar was dead and was made heir to the throne; became king but ruled badly; Odin came to court in disguise to test his behaviour and was tied to a spit between two fires; Geirrod got his just desserts – Odin was furious and caused him to trip on his own sword and kill himself. *Personality:* wicked; unjust; sly; ungrateful. **Page 36.**

GEIRROD (gay-rod).ii. *Category:* Giant. *Family Status:* two d. Gjalp, Greip. *Career:* sworn enemy of the gods; captured Loki who was wearing Freyja's falcon skin; made him promise to bring Thor to him unarmed; his daughters tried to kill Thor on his way to their hall; they failed; daughters killed by Thor; attacked Thor with red-hot iron but the god threw it back and he was killed. *Personality:* evil; scheming; over-confident. *Distinguishing Features:* very large. **Page 27.**

GERD (gird). *Category:* Giantess. *Family Status:* m. Freyr. *Career:* Frost Giantess; born enemy to the gods; spotted by Freyr when he looked at Jotunheim from Odin's throne; wooed for Freyr by Skirnir; indifferent to Freyr's love; agreed to meet Freyr after Skirnir made threats on her father's life; strength of Freyr's love melted her icy heart and she married him; went to live in Asgard and was happy. *Personality:* naturally cold; frigid; became loving. *Distinguishing Features:* v. large; shining beauty. **Page 21.**

GIANTS/GIANTESSES. *Category:* supernatural beings. *Career:* may be Frost, Fire, or Mountain Giants; with a few exceptions they are enemies to the gods (esp. Thor); war-making, cheating or fooling the gods are their favourite pastimes; their stronghold, Utgard, is said to be either in the barren mountains of Jotunheim, East of Midgard, or beyond the Ocean; *Personality:* Frost Giants extremely cold characters; Fire Giants hot-tempered; Mountain Giants hard as rocks; all short-tempered; quick to physical violence. *Distinguishing Features:* enormous size; frosty, fiery or rocky appearance, depending on type. *Supernatural Attributes:* strength equalling the gods'; shape-changing ability. **Page 7, 9, 11, 23, 25, 27, 28, 29, 30, 31, 32, 33, 38.**

GILLING (ghill-ing). *Category:* Giant. *Career:* he and his wife killed by evil Dwarfs, Fjalar and Galar for no recorded reason; his brother, Suttung went to avenge his death and got Mead of Poetry as a pay-off; his other brother Braugi was used by Odin to obtain the Mead by a trick. *Personality:* gullible. *Distinguishing Features:* huge stature. **Page 33.**

GIUKI (gyook-ee). *Category:* human. *Family Status:* m. Grimhild; one s. Gunnar; one d. Gudrun. *Career:* King of the Nibelungs; party to his wife's plan to get Sigurd's treasure by making him forget Brynhild and marry his own daughter, Gudrun. *Personality:* weak. **Page 35.**

GRID (greed). *Category:* Giantess. *Career:* ally of the gods; warned naive Thor against Geirrod when he stayed at her house with Loki on his way to Geirrod's hall; gave Thor a magic belt and iron gauntlets. *Personality:* wise; kind. *Distinguishing Features:* v. big. **Page 27.**

GRIMHILD (grim-hild). *Category:* human. *Family Status:* m. Giuki; one s. Gunnar; one d. Gudrun. *Career:* Queen of the Nibelungs; caught in the curse of Andvari's gold; desired to get the gold from Sigurd; gave him a love potion so he forgot Brynhild, his betrothed, and married her daughter, Gudrun; got the gold but brought the curse down on her family and there followed many violent deaths. *Personality:* grasping; opportunist; ambitious; domineering. **Page 35.**

GRIMNIR (grim-near). *Category:* human/god. *Career:* Odin in disguise; magician; form taken by Odin when visiting King Geirrod's court to test his treatment of guests; was extremely badly treated – tied to a spit between two fires; was pitied by Geirrod's son, who gave him a drink; burst out of this disguise; despatched Geirrod by making him stumble onto his own sword. *Personality:* apparently amiable and wise. *Distinguishing Features:* wore blue cloak and large hat; dogs would not bark at him. *Supernatural Attributes:* magician; possessed all the powers of Odin. **Page 36.**

GUDRUN (good-roon). *Category:* human. *Family Status:* d. of King Giuki and Queen Grimhild; m. Sigurd; m. Alti; several sons. *Career:* entered her mother's plot to marry Sigurd for his treasure; thus became victim of curse of Andvari's gold; Sigurd killed by jealous Brynhild; married Alti and made him kill Sigurd's murderers; Alti killed Gudrun's brothers to have all the gold for himself; she arranged Alti's death in revenge; met a violent death herself, as did all her sons; these deaths ended Andvari's curse. *Personality:* strong-willed; ambitious; unscrupulous. **Page 35.**

GULLFAXI (gool-fax-ee) "Golden Mane". *Category:* supernatural animal. *Career:* steed of the Giant Hrungnir; took part in a race with Odin on Sleipnir; passed into Thor's hands when the god slew Hrungnir; was desired by Odin, but Thor gave him to his own son, Magni. *Distinguishing Features:* superb horse with golden mane. *Supernatural Attributes:* could gallop through air. **Page 28.**

GULLINBURSTI (gool-in-burst-ee) "Golden Bristles". *Category:* supernatural animal. *Career:* made by Dwarfs, Brokk and Eitri; given to Loki, who gave it to Freyr; pulled Freyr's chariot and became his symbol. *Distinguishing Features:* a boar with golden bristles. *Personality:* fierce. *Supernatural Attributes:* fantastic running speed. **Page 26.**

GULLTOP (gool-top). *Category:* supernatural animal. *Career:* Heimdall's mount. *Distinguishing Features:* magnificent horse with golden mane. *Supernatural Attributes:* great speed; flying powers. **Page 19.**

GULLVEIG (gool-vague). *Category:* Vanir goddess. *Career:* mistress of magic; seeress; catalyst in war between the gods; she visited the Aesir and boasted about her magic skills but would not tell her secrets; was murdered and thrown on the fire by the Aesir; by her magic powers she emerged unscathed; the Aesir tried to

burn her twice more but finally allowed her to go free; given a new name, Heid, meaning Gleaming One; she recounted her shameful treatment to the Vanir and ensuing argument with the Aesir caused war between the gods. *Personality:* boastful; infuriating. *Supernatural Attributes:* gift of prophecy; magic powers; healing ability. **Page 22.**

GUNNAR (goon-ar). *Category:* human. *Family Status:* s. of King Giuki and Queen Grimhild; m. Brynhild. *Career:* desired Brynhild; took advantage of his mother's plan to marry his sister to Sigurd to get Brynhild for himself; used Sigurd to woo Brynhild. *Personality:* mother-dominated; insensitive. **Page 35.**

GUNNLOD (goon-lod). *Category:* Giantess. *Family Status:* d. of Suttung. *Career:* had lonely task of guarding the Mead of Poetry in underground cavern; poor girl fooled by Odin who courted her in his disguise as a handsome Giant; was persuaded to give him a sip of Mead; he took it all and disappeared; she was heart-broken; had to face Suttung's extreme anger. *Personality:* easily taken in; not too bright. *Distinguishing Features:* enormous build. **Page 33.**

GYLFI (ghill-vee). *Category:* human. *Career:* King of Sweden; lost a large chunk of his kingdom when he got involved with goddess, Gefion; she was in disguise as a beggarwoman; he talked with her all night and was so impressed by her wisdom that he offered her as much of his kingdom as she could plough with four oxen in a day as a reward; was taught a resounding lesson when Gefion used supernatural oxen and dragged away a huge tract of land; she towed it to Denmark, where it became island of Zealand; left a hole in Sweden which became Lake Malar. *Personality:* caring; well-meaning but unwise. **Page 32-33.**

HARBARD (hah-bard). *Category:* human/god. *Career:* ferryman; disguise chosen by Odin to get his own back on Thor for not giving him the Giant Hrungnir's horse; refused to carry Thor across river, told him lies about his family and drove him to a fury. *Personality:* irritating; unpleasant. **Page 15.**

HATI (hah-tee). *Category:* supernatural animal. *Family Status:* s. of Giantess of Iron Wood. *Career:* chasing Moon across sky; destined to catch and swallow Moon at Ragnarok. *Personality:* single-minded; relentless. *Distinguishing Features:* he is a huge wolf. *Supernatural Attributes:* runs through the air. **Page 11, 39.**

HEID (hade). See **GULLVEIG.**

HEIMDALL (hame-dall). *Category:* Vanir god. *Family Status:* s. of nine maidens, possibly daughters of Aegir and Ran. *Career:* guardian of Bifrost, the Rainbow bridge between Asgard and Midgard; warned the gods of the approach of strangers; constant enemy to Loki; founder of the breeds of thrall, farmer and noble when he visited Earth in disguise as Rig and gave three sons to three families typical of the three types. *Personality:* noble;

serious-minded. *Supernatural Attributes:* super-fine hearing and sight – can hear the grass grow and see for a hundred miles; needs little sleep; possesses gold-maned stallion, Gulltop, who can fly. **Page 9, 17, 18, 25, 29, 39.**

HEL (hell). *Category:* supernatural being. *Family Status:* d. of Loki and Giantess Angrboda. *Career:* enemy to the gods; banished to Land of the Dead (also called Hel) when the Norns warned the gods against her; became Queen of the Dead and ruled over those who died other than in battle; said Balder could return from the dead if everything in the Nine Worlds mourned for him – it was her father who would not cry so she could refuse to release Balder; she will lead dead souls against the gods at Ragnarok. *Personality:* cold; stern; unforgiving. *Distinguishing Features:* horrifically deformed – beautiful woman to the waist, dead and rotting below. **Page 9, 17, 24, 37, 39.**

HERMOD (hair-mod). *Category:* Aesir god. *Family Status:* s. of Odin. *Career:* unexceptional until Frigg needed a volunteer to visit Hel to try and get Balder back; he successfully bargained with Hel for release of Balder, as long as every living thing would mourn for him; foiled when Loki, disguised as Giantess, refused to weep. *Personality:* honourable; brave. **Page 37.**

HILDISVINI (hill-dee-sveen-ee). *Category:* supernatural animal. *Family Status:* belonged to Freyja. *Career:* servant and symbol to Freyja; lent his form to Ottar when he went with Freyja to visit Giantess Hyndla to obtain list of Ottar's ancestors. *Distinguishing Features:* he is a boar. *Supernatural Attributes:* can travel at great speed. **Page 32.**

HJORDIS (hyaw-deess). *Category:* human. *Family Status:* d. of Hreidmar; m. Sigmund; one s. Sigurd. *Career:* Sigurd died before birth of Sigmund; mother and son cared for by her brother, Regin. *Personality:* quiet; submissive. **Page 34.**

HOD (hod). *Category:* Aesir god. *Family Status:* s. of Odin and Frigg. *Career:* little known of his career – hampered by blindness; unfairly used by Loki to murder Balder; Loki gave him poison mistletoe dart to join in game of throwing things at Balder to see how they bounced safely off him; Loki guided Hod's aim and dart killed Balder; although innocent of evil intent, Hod was killed by Odin's son, Vali, in revenge; justice will be done when Hod returns from dead after Ragnarok to be among new gods. *Personality:* solitary; outsider; *Distinguishing Features:* blindness. **Page 37, 39.**

HONIR (ho-near). *Category:* Aesir god. *Career:* great warrior; went to live in Vanaheim when gods swapped leaders after their war; Vanir not particularly impressed by him – he was strong but not clever; Mimir (his companion) suffered for his shortcomings; Vanir cut off Mimir's head and sent it back to Odin to show their disappointment. *Personality:* aggressive; none too bright. *Distinguishing Features:* warrior dress. **Page 22.**

HREIDMAR (hrade-mar). *Category:* human. *Family Status:* three s. Regin, Fafnir, Otter. *Career:* farmer; magician; Otter, disguised as an otter, was unwittingly killed by Loki, who was visiting Earth with Odin and Honir; Hreidmar demanded large sum of gold in compensation; Loki fetched him the treasure of Andvari the Dwarf; Andvari cursed the gold, esp. a gold ring; the curse took effect when Fafnir killed Hreidmar in his greed for the gold; this was the start of long chain of death and violence associated with Andvari's gold. *Personality:* shrewd; avaricious. **Page 34.**

HRUNGNIR (hroong-near). *Category:* Giant. *Career:* challenged Odin to a race; their horses evenly matched; ended up in Asgard having a friendly drink together; he got drunk and rowdy and thrown out by Thor; arranged single combat with Thor; threw whetstone at Thor but killed by Mjollnir; body fell on top of Thor and had to be removed by Thor's son Magni; pieces of shattered whetstone lodged in Thor's head, causing headaches. *Personality:* competitive; given to over-indulgence in alcohol. *Distinguishing Features:* great size. **Page 28.**

HUGINN (hoog-in) "Thought" and **MUNINN** (moon-in) "Memory". *Category:* supernatural animals. *Career:* news reporters to Odin; they fly through the Nine Worlds collecting information, then whisper it in  Odin's ears; when not investigating, are to be found on Odin's shoulders. *Personality:* nosy; tireless. *Distinguishing Features:* they are giant ravens. **Page 12.**

HYMIR (him-ear). *Category:* Giant. *Family Status:* m. Tyr's mother. *Career:* best-known for obstructing Thor and Tyr when they came to fetch a cauldron for Aegir to make ale in for the gods; he and Thor went fishing after Thor polished off all the meat there was in the house; got a fright when Thor attracted Jormungand to his hook and there was a mighty struggle; reluctant to let Thor have the cauldron he requested; said the god could have it if he could break a magic glass Hymir possessed; Thor broke magic spell, and glass, by throwing it at Hymir's head; Hymir gave him the cauldron with bad grace; sent many-headed giants after the gods to attack them, but Thor dealt with them. *Personality:* grumpy; ill-will towards gods; grudging. *Distinguishing Features:* enormous build. **Page 31.**

HYNDLA (hinnd-la). *Category:* Giantess. *Career:* antipathy towards gods; keeper of complete list of Ottar's ancestors; famed for her unhelpfulness when Freyja came to her wanting list; was persuaded to hand list over, but would not give Ottar a sip of magic Memory Beer so he could remember the names; went too far in antagonizing the goddess; Freyja lost her temper and threw ring of fire round Hyndla, which closed in on her; Giantess

gave in and handed over Beer; placed curse on Ottar, but ineffective as he had Freyja's protection. *Personality:* bad-tempered; obstructive; strong instinct for self-preservation. *Distinguishing Features:* gigantic proportions. *Supernatural Attributes:* possession of magic Memory Beer. **Page 32.**

HYRROKIN (hirro-kin). *Category:* Giantess. *Career:* friend to the gods; renowned for pushing Balder and Nanna's funeral boat out to sea; nobody else could move it as it was so laden with treasure. *Personality:* sympathetic; helpful. *Distinguishing Features:* hugeness. **Page 37.**

IDUNN (id-doon). *Category:* Aesir goddess. *Family Status:* m. to Bragi. *Career:* keeper of golden apples that keep the gods young; led by Loki into near-disaster when he tricked her into leaving Asgard with her apples;  this was part of a deal he had made with the Giant Thiazi to escape from his clutches; she was captured and imprisoned by Thiazi; gods started to grow old and weak without her apples to eat; was rescued by Loki, flying in Freyja's falcon skin; he turned her into a nut to carry her in his beak; brought her back safely to Asgard; Thiazi followed and was killed by gods. *Personality:* good; responsible; naive. *Distinguishing Features:* young and beautiful. *Supernatural Attributes:* responsibility for golden apples of youth. **Page 13, 25.**

JARL (yarl). *Category:* human. *Family Status:* s. of Fathir and Mothir, given them by Heimdall; m. Enna; many children. *Career:* brought up as son of wealthy parents; grew handsome and strong; when out hunting one day, was met by Heimdall, who told him some of the secrets of the gods so he became esp. wise; Heimdall said he had a right to win lands and rule men and this is what he did; his descendants were the class of nobles. *Personality:* valiant; noble. **Page 19.**

JARNSAXA (yarn-sax-a). *Category:* Giantess. *Family Status:* lo. of Thor; two s. Magni and Modi. *Career:* friendly to gods; Thor's mistress; cared for their sons. *Personality:* kind; maternal. *Distinguishing Features:* large size. **Page 29.**

JORMUNGAND (yore-mun-gand). *Category:* monster. *Family Status:* s. of Loki and Giantess, Angrboda. *Career:* trouble-making enemy of the gods; thrown into Ocean by Odin, after warning from Norns that he was a danger;  grew bigger and bigger until he circled the Earth and could take his own tail in his mouth; posed great threat to sailors who ventured into deep waters; was once

hooked by Thor when he was fishing with Hymir; there was a great struggle, but Thor bashed him on the head and he retreated; still holds grudge against Thor and they are destined to meet again at Ragnarok; it is predicted that Thor will kill him, only to die himself from Jormungand's poison. *Personality:* malevolent; menacing; danger to humans and gods. *Distinguishing Features:* gigantic serpent – called the World Serpent. *Supernatural Attributes:* fatal venom. **Page 9, 17, 24, 31, 39.**

JORTH (yorth) "Earth". *Category:* goddess. *Family Status:* lo. of Odin; one s. Thor. *Career:* Mother goddess; could simply be Frigg by another name. **Page 14.**

KARL (karl). *Category:* human. *Family Status:* s. of Afi and Amma, given to them by Heimdall; many sons. *Career:* raised as farm-owner; destined to be ancestor of all farm-owners. *Personality:* down to earth; hard-working; practical. **Page 19.**

KOBOLDS (co-bolds). *Category:* supernatural beings. *Career:* live near humans in barns and stables; sometimes helpful, sometimes a pest depending on how they are treated. *Personality:* elusive; mischievous. *Distinguishing Features:* small; human-shaped. **Page 7.**

KVASIR (kvah-seer). *Category:* human. *Career:* fashioned from spittle of the gods when they all spat into jar to seal the peace after war between Aesir and Vanir; inherited wisdom of the gods and was consulted for his good advice throughout the world; treacherously murdered by Dwarfs Fjalar and Galar; they brewed the Mead of Poetry from his blood; the Mead inspired wisdom and poetry in those who drank it; it passed into the hands of the Giant, Suttung, and eventually Odin obtained it for the gods by trickery. *Personality:* wise; trusting. *Supernatural Attributes:* wisdom of the gods. **Page 33.**

LAUFEY (lowf-ee). *Category:* Giantess. *Family Status:* m. Farbauti; s. incl. Loki. *Career:* mother of Loki. **Page 17.**

LIF (leaf) and **LIFTHRASIR** (leaf-thrass-ear). *Category:* humans. *Family Status:* m. to each other. *Career:* escaped into branches of Yggdrasil at Ragnarok and survived to re-populate Earth. *Personality:* strong survival instinct; opportunists. **Page 39.**

LIGHT ELVES. See **ELVES.**

LOGI (lo-ghee). *Category:* Giant. *Career:* enemy to the gods; well-known for incident when Thor and Loki visited Utgard when his form was borrowed by Fire to beat Loki in eating contest; Fire consumes everything, so won the contest for Giants. *Personality:* competitive. *Distinguishing Features:* great size. **Page 30.**

LOKI (lo-kee). *Category:* Giant/god. *Family Status:* s. of Giants Farbauti and Laufey; lo. of Angrboda and had three children, Jormungand, Fenrir, Hel; m. Sigyn and had two sons, Vali and Narvi. *Career:* blood-brother to Odin; lived in Asgard and had god-like status; loved adventures, mischief, trickery and disguise; amused the gods (except Heimdall); went with them on adventures – to Utgard with Thor; to Earth with Odin and Honir; provoked Andvari's curse by stealing his gold; always in trouble with Giants; compromised others to save himself – caused kidnapping of Idunn and got Thor into danger with the Giant Geirrod; produced magic, eight-legged horse, Sleipnir, while in disguise as a mare; got treasures from the Dwarfs; gradually embittered as gods tired of his behaviour and began to laugh at him; jealous of Balder and caused his death; prevented Balder's return from dead by refusing to weep for him; avoided gods after this but later turned up at a feast and made spiteful speech against them; ran off but was caught; tied to rocks; a serpent that dropped venom on his face placed overhead; Sigyn tried to catch poison but when it hit him he writhed and the Earth shook; he was fated to break free and fight the gods at Ragnarok. **Personality:** mischievous, becoming evil; daring; annoying; strong instinct for self-preservation. *Distinguishing Features:* small; handsome; agile; often called Shape-Changer. *Supernatural Attributes:* great gift for shape-changing. **Page 17, 19, 23, 24, 25, 26, 27, 29, 30, 34, 37, 38, 39.**

MAGNI (mag-nee). *Category:* god. *Family Status:* s. of Thor and Giantess Jarnsaxa. *Career:* extremely strong from birth; at only three years old he rescued Thor who was trapped under body of the Giant Hrungnir; Thor gave him Hrungnir's horse, Gold Mane, in thanks; he will survive Ragnarok and inherit Thor's hammer; will be one of the new gods. *Personality:* brave and bold. **Page 28, 39**

MIMIR (mee-meer). *Category:* Aesir god. *Career:* guardian of Well of Mimir in Jotunheim, fountain of all wisdom; was v. wise; gave Odin a sip from the well, at the cost of one of his eyes; was sent with Honir to live with Vanir when gods exchanged leaders after the war between them; became victim of Vanir's disappointment in Honir, who was useless if separated from Mimir; showed their disapproval by cutting off Mimir's head and sending it back to Odin; Odin preserved it and gave it the power of speech; placed head back by Mimir's Well so it could still be consulted. *Personality:* v. knowledgeable; good teacher. *Distinguishing Features:* existed as a head only after being beheaded by Vanir. *Supernatural Attributes:* wisdom and talking ability even after head cut off. **Page 9, 22, 23.**

MODI (mode-ee). *Category:* god. *Family Status:* s. of Thor and Giantess Jarnsaxa. *Career:* no known deeds of note; his time is in the future after Ragnarok, when he will be one of the new leaders; he and his brother, Magni, will recover Thor's hammer and help world to recover. *Personality:* brave; good. **Page 39.**

MOON. *Category:* human. *Family Status:* s. of Mundulfari. *Career:* named after the planet by his father because he was v. beautiful; gods thought this was a cheek and took him away as punishment; made to drive chariot pulling the moon; pursued by terrible wolf Hati who wants to catch and destroy him. **Page 11.**

MOTHIR (moe-theer) "Mother". *Family Status:* m. Fathir; one s. Jarl, given to them as a gift from Heimdall. *Career:* nobleman's wife; chosen by Heimdall to care for Jarl, who was to be ancestor of all nobles. *Personality:* motherly. **Page 19.**

MUNDULFARI (moon-dool-farri). See **MOON.**

MUNINN (mun-in). See **HUGINN.**

NANNA (nan-ah). *Category:* Aesir goddess. *Family Status:* m. Balder; one s. Forseti. *Career:* loving wife; died of broken heart when Balder killed and cremated with him on funeral ship; arrived in Niflheim with Balder. *Personality:* gentle; loving. **Page 16, 37.**

NARVI (nar-vee). *Category:* god. *Family Status:* s. of Loki and Sigyn. *Career:* cut short by the gods when they killed him to punish Loki; was torn apart by his brother, Vali , whom gods turned into a wolf; his entrails used to bind Loki. *Personality:* unfortunate. **Page 17, 38.**

NIDHOGG (nid-hog). *Category:* monster. *Career:* enemy to the gods; attempted to destroy world by gnawing roots of Yggdrasil to kill it; guardian of Spring of Hvergelmir in Niflheim; his role after Ragnarok is to attack the corpses of wrong-doers in Nastrond. *Personality:* deliberately evil; bloodthirsty. *Distinguishing Features:* he is a dreadful dragon. **Page 9.**

NIGHT. *Category:* Giantess. *Family Status:* one s. Day. *Career:* drove horse-drawn chariot round the world once every 24 hours, bringing night. *Personality:* consistent; dutiful. *Distinguishing Features:* brought darkness. **Page 11.**

NJORD (nyord). *Category:* Vanir god. *Family Status:* one s. Freyr; one d. Freyja; m. Giantess Skadi. *Career:* god of the sea; went to live with Aesir in the exchange of leaders after war between the gods; chosen by Giantess Skadi when she was allowed to pick a husband from looking at the gods' feet; unsuccessful marriage because Skadi could not stand the sea and he could not stand her native mountains so they lived apart; helped Freyr woo his wife, Gerd. *Personality:* noble; wise; stubborn. **Page 18, 20, 21, 25.**

NORNS (nornz). *Category:* goddesses (three). *Career:* spinning destinies of humans and gods; they know everyone's Fate; sometimes known as Past, Present and Future; tend the Well of Urd in Asgard and water Yggdrasil; warned gods against Loki's brood. *Personality:* all-knowing; incorruptible. *Distinguishing Features:* v. old and wise. *Supernatural Attributes:* ability to see the future; power over lives of humans and gods. **Page 9, 24.**

NORTH. *Category:* Dwarf. *Career:* holding up the sky with Dwarfs South, East and West. **Page 11.**

OD (odd). *Category:* god. *Family Status:* m. Freyja. *Career:* he has abandoned Freyja, who mourns for him. *Personality:* apparently unfaithful and unreliable. **Page 20.**

ODIN (oh-din). *Category:* Aesir god. *Family Status:* m. Frigg; two s, Balder, Hod; many lo. incl. Rind – one s. Vali; Grid – one s. Vidar; all gods are his offspring. *Career:* King of the gods; father of all other gods and creator of humans; called Allfather; god of war; v. wise – gave up one eye to drink from Well of Mimir; sacrificed himself, died and was reborn to gain secrets of the dead; obtained the Runes and taught them to mankind; keeps watch on everything that happens in the Nine Worlds; enjoys visiting Earth in disguise; his servants, the Valkyries, choose brave warriors for him to entertain in his hall, Vallhalla. *Personality:* arrogant; stern; can be jealous and unpleasant. *Distinguishing Features:* often to be seen with the two ravens, Huginn and Muninn on his shoulders. *Supernatural Attributes:* all-seeing and all-knowing; shape-changing. **Page 12, 13, 14, 15, 16, 20, 21, 22, 24, 28, 33, 34, 36, 37, 39.**

OTTAR (ot-ar). *Category:* human. *Family Status:* lo. of Freyja. *Career:* prince; devoted to Freyja; came to Freyja's notice, she fell in love and came to Midgard to be with him; entered contest with Angantyr to decide quarrel over his throne; had to list all his ancestors correctly; Freyja turned him into her boar, Hildisvini, to visit Giantess Hyndla who had the list; with difficulty, Freyja obtained list and Memory Beer to help him remember it; Ottar cursed by Hyndla, but protected by Freyja and won the throne. *Personality:* single-minded; non-violent. *Supernatural Attributes:* Freyja's special protection. **Page 32.**

RAGING WARRIOR see **VALKYRIES**

RAN (ran). *Category:* Vanir goddess. *Family Status:* m. Aegir; nine daughters. *Career:* sea goddess; netted drowning victims and dragged them to sea-bed; entertained them in her hall; held feast at which Loki insulted gods. *Personality:* variable, like the sea; unpredictable; stormy temper. **Page 18, 34, 38.**

RATATOSK (rat-ah-tosk). *Category:* supernatural animal. *Career:* running up and down trunk of Yggdrasil, trading insults between Nidhogg and eagle that sits in top branches. *Personality:* spiteful gossip; trouble-maker. *Distinguishing Features:* he is a squirrel. **Page 9.**

REGIN (ray-ghin). *Category:* human. *Family Status:* s. of Hreidmar. *Career:* farmer; helped tie up Odin, Loki and Honir after they killed one of his brothers; was refused his share of Andvari's gold after his brother, Fafnir, killed their father to get it; got revenge by bringing up his nephew, Sigurd, to kill Fafnir, which he did; then became affected by the curse on the gold, turned against Sigurd and planned to kill him; was killed by Sigurd in self-defence. *Personality:* good and kind until tainted by curse; then greedy and ruthless. **Page 34.**

RIG (rig). *Category:* human/god. *Family Status:* gave s. to Edda (Thrall); Amma (Karl); Mothir (Jarl). *Career:* human form taken by Heimdall when he visited Earth to found races of nobles, farm-owners and thralls. *Personality:* friendly; welcome guest; good judge of character. **Page 19.**

ROSKVA (rosk-va). See **THIALFI.**

SHAKER and **SHRIEKING**. See **VALKYRIES.**

SIF (siff). *Category:* Aesir goddess. *Family Status:* m. Thor. *Career:* goddess of harvest, fruitfulness and plenty; had her hair cut off by Loki; she replaced it with magic spun-gold which grew like hair, made by the Dwarfs. *Personality:* generous; somewhat vain. *Distinguishing Features:* long, gold hair. **Page 15, 26.**

SIGMUND (sig-mund). *Category:* human. *Family Status:* m. Hjordis; one s. Sigurd. *Career:* died before Sigurd born. **Page 34.**

SIGURD (sig-urd). *Category:* human. *Family Status:* grands. of Hreidmar; s. of Hjordis and Sigmund; lo. of Brynhild; m. Gudrun. *Career:* brave and adventurous but became entangled in curse of Andvari's gold; reared by his uncle, Regin, to kill his other uncle, Fafnir, for murdering Hreidmar to get the gold; Fafnir had turned into a dragon, but Sigurd killed him and ate his heart; rescued Valkyrie Brynhild from her enchanted sleep; was to marry her, but given a love potion by Grimhild of the Nibelungs, which made him forget Brynhild and marry Grimhild's daughter, Gudrun; thus the gold came into the hands of the Nibelungs; was murdered on jealous Brynhild's orders. *Personality:* courageous; good. *Supernatural Attributes:* could understand the speech of birds. **Page 34.**

SIGYN (sig-in). *Category:* goddess. *Family Status:* m. Loki; two s. Vali, Narvi. *Career:* faithful and loving wife to Loki, despite his bad behaviour; remained loyal even during his punishment – held bowl to try to keep poison off Loki's face. *Personality:* warm and loving; unquestioningly loyal. **Page 17, 38.**

SKADI (skah-dee). *Category:* Giantess. *Family Status:* d. of Thiazi; m. Njord. *Career:* great huntress; came to demand compensation when they killed her father; was offered one of the gods in marriage; to be chosen from their feet; chose Njord's feet; unhappy marriage as she hated the sea and he hated mountains so they were not happy anywhere together; eventually they separated; given gift of laughter by Odin; placed snake above Loki to drip poison on him as part of his punishment. *Personality:* brave; independent. *Associations:* the word "Scandinavia" comes from the name Skadi. **Page 18, 25, 38.**

SKIRNIR (skeer-near). *Category:* god. *Career:* servant to Freyr; had the arm-ring Gleipnir made by the Dwarfs; made dangerous mission to Jotunheim to woo Gerd for Freyr; was given Freyr's magic sword in return; this was destined to be Freyr's downfall as he will not have sword at Ragnarok. *Personality:* daring; loyal. *Supernatural Attributes:* owner of Freyr's sword which moves through the air of its own accord. **Page 21, 25.**

SKOLL (skol). *Category:* supernatural animal. *Family Status:* s. of Witch of Iron Wood. *Career:* chasing Sun across sky in an attempt to swallow her; at Ragnarok he will succeed. *Personality:* evil singlemindedness; ferocious. *Distinguishing Features:* he is a monstrous wolf. **Page 11.**

SKRYMIR (skree-meer). *Category:* Giant. *Career:* disguise adopted by Utgard-Loki, King of the Giants, to annoy Thor's party on their way to Utgard; deliberately disturbed their sleep by snoring; sealed their food bag by magic so they could not eat; murder attempts by Thor failed because he protected himself by magic. *Personality:* unpleasant; exasperating. *Distinguishing Features:* hugeness. *Supernatural Attributes:* shapechanging; magic powers. **Page 30.**

SLEIPNIR (slape-near). *Category:* supernatural animal. *Family Status:* s. of Loki and Svadilfari. *Career:* born from Loki while in disguise as a mare; Loki gave him to Odin as peace offering; carried Odin on many adventures. *Personality:* brave; loyal. *Distinguishing Features:* he is a white, eight-legged horse. *Supernatural Attributes:* can gallop with equal ease over land, sea or air. **Page 12, 23, 28.**

SOUTH. *Category:* Dwarf. *Career:* holding up the sky with Dwarfs, North, West and East. **Page 11.**

SUN. *Category:* human. *Family Status:* d. of Mundulfari; one d. yet to be born. *Career:* named after the planet by her father as she was so beautiful; the gods found this presumptuous and carried her away as punishment; made her drive chariot of the sun; pursued by giant wolf Skoll who is trying to catch her; Skoll will succeed when Raganarok comes but her daughter will survive and light the new world. **Page 11.**

SURT (sert) "Black". *Category:* supernatural being. *Career:* guarding gates of Muspell and ruling fiery beings who live there; at Ragnarok he will lead his hordes out of Muspell against the gods; he will set the 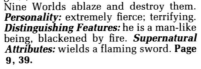 Nine Worlds ablaze and destroy them. *Personality:* extremely fierce; terrifying. *Distinguishing Features:* he is a man-like being, blackened by fire. *Supernatural Attributes:* wields a flaming sword. **Page 9, 39.**

SUTTUNG (soot-ung). *Category:* Giant. *Family Status:* brother to Gilling and

Braugi; one d. Gunnlod. *Career:* went to avenge Gilling's death when he was killed by Dwarfs; took pay-off of Mead of Poetry instead; placed Mead in cavern with Gunnlod on guard; boasted about the Mead; would not give Odin (in disguise as the Giant Bolverk) a sip as Braugi had promised, in payment for work Odin did; then was furious when Odin stole the Mead. *Personality:* bragging; foolish. *Distinguishing Features:* vastness. **Page 33.**

SVADILFARI (svad-ill-far-ee). *Category:* animal. *Family Status:* belonged to a Rock Giant; mated with Loki (in disguise as a mare); one s. Sleipnir. *Career:* worked for the Rock Giant; esp. known for carrying stones from quarry to rebuild Asgard's wall; used by Loki to prevent Giant completing his contract and carrying off his rewards – Loki took form of a mare and lured him into woods; Giant could not finish work without him. *Personality:* hard-working; amorous. **Page 22, 23.**

SYR (seer) "sow". See **FREYJA**

THIALFI (thyalf-ee). *Category:* human. *Family Status:* brother to Roskva. *Career:* poor peasant; his family gave shelter to Thor and Loki, on their journey to Utgard; greed got the better of him and he broke thighbone of one of Thor's goats (Thor had killed them to provide meat) to suck the marrow, though expressly forbidden to touch them; he and Roskva taken as servants by Thor in recompense; took part in race with Giant in Utgard, but lost. *Personality:* incautious. **Page 30.**

THIAZI (thyah-zee). *Category:* Giant. *Family Status:* one d. Skadi. *Career:* antigod activity; tormented Odin, Honir and Loki on a trip to Earth by taking disguise as eagle and using magic to prevent their meat cooking; attacked by Loki so carried him off and made him promise to bring Idunn and her golden apples in return for releasing him; Loki kept bargain and Thiazi imprisoned Idunn; gods grew old and frail without apples of youth; Loki rescued Idunn; Thiazi flew after him in eagle form; met his death when he followed Loki into Asgard and was set upon by the gods; his eyes put in the sky as stars by Odin to appease Skadi when she came for revenge. *Personality:* sly; aggressive; over-confident. *Distinguishing Features:* v. big. *Supernatural Attributes:* shapechanging. **Page 25.**

THOR (thaw). *Category:* Aesir god. *Family Status:* s. of Odin and Jorth; m. Sif; many lo. incl. Jarnsaxa (two s. Modi, Magni); Giantess (one d. Thrud). *Career:* thunder-god; god of law and order; great warrior; Defender of Asgard; v. popular; loved fighting, feasting and drinking; many adventures – greatest enemy of the Giants, though they taught him a lesson when he visited Utgard; controlled storms on Earth; sometimes a figure of fun to other gods for his simplicity. *Personality:* trusting; good-natured, despite quick temper; not too brainy; v. confident of his superior strength. *Distinguishing Features:* wild red hair and beard; always in battle-dress; drove chariot pulled by giant goats. *Supernatural Attributes:* the hammer, Mjollnir; belt that doubled his strength; iron gauntlets for grasping any weapon. **Page 2, 12, 14-15, 17, 26, 27, 28, 29, 30, 31, 38, 39.**

THRALL (thrawl). *Category:* human. *Family Status:* s. of Ai and Edda, given to them by Heimdall; many children. *Career:* poor labourer; destined to be ancestor of all landless labourers. *Personality:* dull; simple. **Page 19.**

THRYM (thrim). *Category:* Giant. *Career:* famed for daring to steal Mjollnir and demand Freyja as his wife as reward for returning it; short-lived glory, though, as Thor and Loki went to Thrym's hall disguised as Freyja (in bridal veil) and bridesmaid; when Mjollnir was produced to bless the bride, Thor grabbed it and killed Thrym and many others. *Personality:* arrogant; daring; unwise. *Distinguishing Features:* huge body. **Page 29.**

TOOTHGNASHER and **TOOTHGRINDER**. *Category:* supernatural animals. *Family Status:* belonged to Thor. *Career:* pulling Thor's chariot across the sky; causing thunder on Earth with their hooves. *Distinguishing Features:* they are enormous, fearsome goats. *Supernatural Attributes:* can be eaten and revived next day by Thor. **Page 15.**

TROLLS. *Category:* supernatural beings. *Career:* enemies to the gods, esp. Thor; fighting wars. *Personality:* bad-tempered; war-like. *Distinguishing Features:* similar to Giants; huge. *Supernatural Attributes:* great strength. **Page 7, 38.**

TYR (tier). *Category:* Aesir god. *Family Status:* s. of Odin. *Career:* god of law and order; guaranteed contracts and agreements; patron of the Thing; called bravest of the gods; most admired for daring to put his hand in Fenrir's mouth when gods were trying to bind the wolf and he demanded sign of good faith that he was not being tricked; it was a trick, of course, and Fenrir bit off Tyr's hand – often called the One-Handed after this. *Personality:* honourable; great integrity; enormous courage. *Distinguishing Features:* one missing hand. **Page 16, 25, 31, 39.**

UTGARD-LOKI: (oot-guard-low-kee). *Category:* Giant. *Career:* King of the Giants; dedicated to fighting gods; notorious for getting the better of Thor when he visited Utgard; took disguise as Skrymir. *Personality:* wily; intelligent. *Distinguishing Features:* gigantic. *Supernatural Attributes:* shape-changing. **Page 30.**

VALI (vah-lee). i. See **NARVI.**

VALI (vah-lee).ii. *Category:* god. *Family Status:* s. of Odin and Giantess, Rind. *Career:* noted for killing Hod **Page 38.**

VALKYRIES (val-kye-reez) "Choosers of the Slain". *Category:* supernatural beings. *Career:* female warrior servants to Odin; directed the course of battles; chose the most valiant warriors to go to Valhalla to be Odin's guests when they were slain; also served food and drink to warriors in Valhalla. *Personality:* fearless; frightening. *Distinguishing Features:* battle-dress when choosing the slain. **Page 12, 29, 36.**

VANIR (vah-near). *Category:* gods. *Family Status:* all children of Odin.

Career: fertility gods; at first antagonistic to Aesir gods, but after war between the two types they co-operated and lived in peace; main leaders – Njord, Freyja, Freyr, Aegir, Ran, Heimdall. *Supernatural Attributes:* magic powers; witchcraft. **Page 6, 9, 18, 20, 21, 22, 23.**

VE (vay) and **VILI** (vill-ee). *Category:* gods. *Family Status:* s. of Bor and Bestla. *Career:* first gods, with Odin, their brother; helped create the Earth and first humans. **Page 10.**

VIDAR (vee-dar). *Category:* god. *Family Status:* s. of Odin and Grid. *Career:* will avenge Odin by killing Fenrir at Ragnarok; will survive and become one of the new leaders of the gods. *Personality:* noble; brave. **Page 39.**

VILI. See **VE.**

WEST. *Category:* Dwarf. *Career:* holding up the sky with Dwarfs North, South and East. **Page 11.**

YMIR (im-meer). *Category:* Giant. *Family Status:* emerged from vapours of melting snow of Niflheim; many children born from his sweat. *Career:* first Frost Giant; appeared in the emptiness known as Ginnungagap; was suckled by giant cow, Audumla; killed by Odin, Vili and Ve; his body used to form the Earth; his bones and teeth became mountains and his blood filled rivers and seas; his skull formed dome of the sky and his brains were clouds. *Personality:* brutal; evil; violent. *Distinguishing Features:* enormous; icy appearance. **Page 10-11.**

PLACES

ALFHEIM (alf-hame) "Land of the Elves". Home of the Light Elves. **Page 8, 9.**

ASGARD (ass-guard). Land of the Aesir gods. **Page 9, 14, 16, 18, 20, 23, 24, 26, 28.**

BILSKIRNIR (bill-skier-near) "Lightning". Thor and Sif's great hall in Asgard. **Page 15.**

BREIDABLIK (brade-a-blick). Balder and Nanna's home in Asgard. **Page 16.**

GINNUNGAGAP (ghin-un-ga-gap). Great emptiness that existed between Muspell and Niflheim before the world began. **Page 10.**

HEL (hell). Land of the Dead. Ruled over by Hel. **Page 8, 24.**

JOTUNHEIM (yot-oon-hame). Mountain home of the Giants. East of Midgard. **Page 8, 9, 28.**

MIDGARD (mid-guard). Home of humans; Earth. **Page 8, 9, 27, 34, 39.**

MUSPELL (moo-spell). Area of fire before Earth was created. **Page 8, 9, 10-11, 39.**

NIDAVELLIR (need-a vell-ear). Home of the Dwarfs. **Page 9.**

NIFLHEIM (niffle-hame). Area of ice and snow in the North before the world existed. **Page 9.**

NOATUN (noah-toon) "Shipyard". Njord's home by the sea. **Page 18.**

OCEAN. Vast stretch of water around Earth; home of Jormungand. **Page 9, 24.**

SESSRUMNIR (sess-room-near) "Many Seats". Freyja's hall in Asgard. **Page 20.**

SVARTALFHEIM (svart-alf-hame) "Land of the Dark Elves". **Page 9.**

UTGARD (oot-guard). Stronghold of the Giants; either in Jotunheim or beyond the Ocean. **Page 9, 30.**

VALASKJALF (val-ah-skyalf) "Shelf of the Slain". One of Odin's halls in Asgard. Home of throne, Hlidskjalf. **Page 12, 21.**

VALHALLA (val-hal-ah) "Hall of the Slain". One of Odin's halls in Asgard. Home of dead heroes. **Page 12.**

VANAHEIM (van-ah-hame). Land of the Vanir gods. **Page 9, 22.**

VIGARD (vee-guard). Huge plain where Ragnarok will take place. **Page 39.**

THINGS

BIFROST (bee-frost). Rainbow bridge between Asgard and Midgard. **Page 9, 19.**

BRISINGAMEN (briss-ing-a-men) "Necklace of the Brisings". Necklace made by four Dwarfs. **Page 20.**

FOUNTAIN OF MIMIR. Well in Midgard into which one of Yggdrasil's roots dips; guarded by the god Mimir; also called Fountain of Knowledge. **Page 9, 22.**

GJALL (gyall). Heimdall's horn. **Page 39.**

GUNGNIR (goong-near). Magic spear belonging to Odin. **Page 12, 26.**

HLIDSKJALF (hlid-skyalf). Odin's throne in Valaskjalf. **Page 12.**

MJOLLNIR (myoll-near). Supernatural hammer. Thor's main weapon and symbol. **Page 15, 26, 27, 28, 29, 30, 31, 39.**

RAGNAROK (rag-na-rock). Great battle at the end of the world. Doom of the gods. **Page 38.**

SKIDBLADNIR (skid-blad-near). Magic ship made by Dwarfs. Belonged to Freyr. **Page 21, 26.**

SPRING OF HVERGELMIR (hvare-ghel-meer). Well in Niflheim into which one of Yggdrasil's roots dives; guarded by the dragon Nidhogg. **Page 9.**

WELL OF URD (oord). Well in Asgard into which one of Yggdrasil's roots plunges; tended by the Norns. **Page 9.**

YGGDRASIL (ig-dra-sill). Giant ash tree which holds the Nine Worlds in position in space. **Page 9, 23, 39.**

47

INDEX

First published in 1986 by Usborne Publishing Ltd, Usborne House, 83-85 Saffron Hill, London EC1N 8RT, England.

Copyright © 1986 Usborne Publishing Ltd.

48

The name Usborne and the device 🐝 are trademarks of Usborne Publishing Ltd. Printed in Great Britain.